RAN
CREEK
GUEST RANCH

RANGER CREEK
GUEST RANCH

REAL LIFE, REAL FAITH

SUE COMISFORD

TATE PUBLISHING
AND ENTERPRISES, LLC

Published by Tate Publishing & Enterprises, LLC
127 E. Trade Center Terrace | Mustang, Oklahoma 73064 USA
1.888.361.9473 | www.tatepublishing.com

Tate Publishing is committed to excellence in the publishing industry. The company reflects the philosophy established by the founders, based on Psalm 68:11,
"The Lord gave the word and great was the company of those who published it."

Book design copyright © 2014 by Tate Publishing, LLC. All rights reserved.
Cover design by Gian philipp Rufin
Interior design by Joana Quilantang

Published in the United States of America

ISBN: 978-1-63063-220-5
1. Biography & Autobiography / General
2. Biography & Autobiography / Personal Memoirs
14.02.06

Dedication

I dedicate this book to my grandchildren. Over the years since we sold the Ranch, we have told and retold the stories about our experiences. Bill and I and our adult children have wonderful memories of the Ranch which I wanted to put down on paper for our grandchildren and future generations to share.

I want my grandchildren to know how faith in God during a difficult time in our life allowed us to take a leap of faith and step out of our comfort zone to realize a dream.

And, I want my grandchildren to hear about this special place known as Ranger Creek Guest Ranch and share in the stories that are near and dear to our hearts.

Acknowledgments

First I want to acknowledge my son, Brandon. Throughout his battle with cancer, he remained strong and determined. His positive attitude and his determination not to let this disease hinder his ability to live a full and meaningful life enabled our family to remain faithful and grow stronger.

It was Brandon that first had the dream of owning a guest ranch. It was through his determination and faith that we were able to loosen our sense of control over our lives and allow ourselves to dream of a future that included moving away from Ohio and moving toward ownership of a guest ranch. Brandon completed the Back Country Horsemanship Course at Hocking College and worked on various guest ranches throughout Colorado. The knowledge he gained through his coursework at Hocking College and his experiences working on guest ranches made Brandon an invaluable asset to Bill as he researched the guest ranch industry, answering questions and acting as a sounding board for ideas and challenges.

Brandon was present when we signed the purchase contracts and worked alongside Bill and me during the rebuilding stage of the Ranch. He worked with Bill to hire the staff and continued to be an integral part of creating the programs and activities that made the Ranch a success. Even after he moved to Virginia, the story of Brandon's battle with cancer became part of the history of our ownership of the Ranch. The challenges our family faced during his battle with cancer enabled Bill and me to pay forward with our affiliation with The Make-A-Wish Foundation in helping other kids fulfill their dreams and with our annual Ranch Rodeo for kids with life threatening illnesses.

Brandon's story and his love for the Ranch inspired me to put these words on paper. Thank you, Brandon, for your inspiration and for your courage without which, the Ranch would only remain a dream. I love you more than you will ever know.

Secondly, I want to acknowledge my husband Bill, my daughter Missy, and my son Shane. From the first moment Bill heard the words, "We could do something like this, Dad," he began the necessary research and planning to ascertain the viability of owning a ranch. His enthusiasm and creativity was contagious and inspired me to join in the dream. He was patient with me during the hard times and the lonely times when I missed my family. Bill's love of the Ranch spilled over to those who met him and without his enthusiasm the Ranch would not have been a success. You have always been my best friend and I love you more each day.

Missy and Shane, although I feel like your lives were drastically changed because we moved to Wyoming and purchased the Ranch, I also know that you loved the Ranch and share in the wonderful memories of our times there. My heart broke when we moved to Wyoming and I missed you each and every day. Your visits always seemed too short but the memories we made while you were there remain some of my favorite memories of the Ranch. I love both of you so much and enjoy being part of your lives here in Ohio.

Additionally, I would like to acknowledge Zack. You have always been an important part of our family and I am as proud of you as I am of my own children. You worked at the Ranch every summer and your contributions and support were invaluable to the success of the Ranch. Your love for the Ranch was evident and I value the memories that we created as a family.

Finally, I would like to acknowledge the staff and the guests. Without you, there would be no memories and therefore no book. The staff worked so hard and each one contributed their own unique character and talents to the everyday activities of the Ranch. I am thankful and very blessed to have known each and every one of you. Our guests are some of the nicest people, and Bill and I both feel that our lives have been enriched by having known you.

Contents

Introduction 13

Our Journey to the Ranch 17

History of the Ranch 27

Rebuilding of the Ranch 33

Horses 47

Staffing of the Ranch 61

Wild Bill 87

Riding Programs and Activities 93

Riding Program 99

The Singing Rangers of the Big Horn Mountains ... 105

Ranger Creek Ranch Rodeo 109

Wildlife 117

Winter at the Ranch 125

Hunting Season 141

Our Guests 145

Life on the Ranch 175

The Final Chapter 191

Ranch Recipes 205

Articles Published About Ranger Creek Guest Ranch ... 213

Introduction

Like many married couples in their early forties working and raising a family, the thought of moving to Wyoming to own and operate a guest ranch was the farthest thing from our mind. Bill and I were busy attending school and church activities with our children and keeping up with our own work and social commitments. Looking back, our lives seemed to come to an abrupt halt with the words, "your son has cancer." Activities and even worries that consumed our minds before hearing those words didn't seem to carry the same importance anymore. Our priorities began to change. Bill and I and our three children were always a close family but this trial in our lives brought us even closer.

After returning from a trip to a guest ranch in Tucson, Arizona, granted by The Special Wish Foundation, Bill and I really started to reevaluate our lives and how we wanted to spend our future years. We were still consumed by hospital visits for treatment for Brandon's illness and concern over our son's health, but we were learning to release the grasp of control over our lives and envision a life of possibilities and change. Our own transformation was influenced by our son's words, "We could do something like this, Dad."

Bill and I searched for over two years for a ranch to purchase. Just when we were about to give up on our search, our realtor persuaded us to look at a ranch located in the Big Horn Mountains of Wyoming. The day that we drove up the lane into Ranger Creek Guest Ranch just seemed right. We felt like we had finally found exactly the ranch that we had been looking for. The Ranch had such character and although it needed considerable improvement, we could see through the disrepair to the possibilities this Ranch provided.

Brandon was there the day we signed the purchase contracts and worked with Bill and me to develop the programs for the Ranch. His dreams for the Ranch and his battle with cancer became the story of the Ranch long after he moved away.

The peaceful nature of the Ranch allowed our family to heal from the battles that led us there in the first place. We learned to embrace and enjoy the experiences provided by living in this remote area among the wildlife that we enjoyed on a daily basis. We enjoyed the quiet nature of the mountain during the winter when no one else was around and enjoyed sharing these surroundings with guests who came to the Ranch from all over the world.

Although the journey was not always easy, our lives have been touched by the people we met along the way and our hearts are full of wonderful memories of these people and this special place known as Ranger Creek Guest Ranch.

As one guest wrote:

> We stumbled into paradise and you graciously let us stay and share your "bit of heaven."
>
> Thank you for making Danielle and I feel so very welcome. This was truly one of those experiences we'll hold onto for a lifetime. I admire

and envy your life here and wish you success,
but most of all peace and happiness here.

Our Journey
to the Ranch

It was born out of a love for the area. It had withstood the depression, a world war and the destruction of a tornado, but it remained a haven for visitors to escape their fast pace lives. They came to the ranch from all over the world to step back in time and to reap the rewards of what this Ranch and its peaceful nature had to offer.

The Ranch was started by Everton and Hazel Foe of Greybull, Wyoming, in 1934. Everton built the Ranch for his dear wife Hazel, who later died of pneumonia. During World War II, the Ranch was shut down. At the end of the war, Glen and Vera Foe purchased the Ranch from his brother and ran it for four years. Vera commented that, "Everton built it well. He had set up a saw mill near the creek to mill the logs."

Ranger Creek Guest Ranch derived its name from a narrow, clear mountain creek that flowed through the Ranch. The tall lodge pole pines that surrounded the Ranch provided the timber for the log lodge and six of the cabins on the property. A small stone building sat adjacent to the lodge.

As Bill and I drove into the Ranch in 1998, we immediately fell in love with the setting of the Ranch. It sat at an elevation of 8300 feet. Surrounded on the back side by tall mountain peaks, the Ranch sat in a high mountain meadow. Tall lodge pole pines lined the lane that led into the Ranch. With our first glimpse of the buildings, we were reminded of an old western movie. The rustic log lodge was framed by a split rail fence and on one end of the lodge the granite fireplace was centered between boxed hinged windows that opened to the outside. An old wagon sat near the flag pole that proudly displayed the American flag whipping in the Wyoming wind. The log guest cabins were sprinkled among the pine trees. Each cabin was unique with its own wooden porch and split rail banister.

Entering the lodge through the thick wooden door, the great room was spacious with hardwood floors and an open log stairway and balcony that led to two rooms upstairs. The open ceiling was enhanced by massive hand hewn beams. The granite fireplace engulfed one end of the room. Glass windows separated the great room from the dining room which was enclosed with a wall of windows that presented a spectacular view of the broad meadow and the mountain peaks that lay beyond it. Two massive wooden tables with chairs provided a comfy setting for guests. Opposite the fireplace were two wooden swinging doors leading to the kitchen. The kitchen, lined with tall wooden cabinets had all the necessities including an awesome six burner cast iron stove. Beyond the kitchen was a spacious storage room and small bathroom.

The wrangler's quarters and tack room were positioned at the bottom of the foothill just beyond the lodge and cabins. A round pen and paddock areas lay at the rear of the tack room.

As Bill and I were shown the cabins and other buildings on the Ranch, we could see that there was a lot of work that needed to be completed to bring this Ranch up to the standards that we desired to provide for our future guests. Bill and I were always up for an adventure and not strangers to hard work, and we could see through the dirt and disrepair to the potential of this great place. The current owners of the Ranch had operated it for seven years and ran hunting camps and weekend stays. After deciding to sell the Ranch the previous year, it had little activity and the signs of disrepair were evident.

This Ranch, with its rich heritage and eventful past had a character all its own. The Ranch had been handed down through generations of individuals who had taken a risk, not for monetary gain, but for a lifestyle that provided more riches than they could ever imagine.

Although our adventure at Ranger Creek Guest Ranch was about to begin, it didn't come easily. Our journey to the Ranch began several years earlier. Bill and I were a typical mid-western couple raising a family in Ohio. We had met in high school and were married shortly after graduation. Bill earned his college degree from The Ohio State University and then became a Certified Public Accountant and I graduated from Central Ohio Technical College and Capital University Law School as a Legal Assistant/Paralegal. At the time, Bill worked for a "big eight" accounting firm and I worked for a local law firm. Our children, Brandon, Melissa (Missy) and Shane attended Worthington Schools.

Our children were typical high school children who loved spending time with their friends and enjoyed participating in sporting activities such as football, lacrosse, and softball. Bill, Brandon, and Shane were also active in the local Boy Scout Troop (B.S.A. Troop 365). Missy and I enjoyed shopping and spending time together. Our family was also active in our local church.

On September 19, 1991, our world was shaken when our oldest son, Brandon, was diagnosed with Stage IV Hodgkin's Disease, a form of cancer. The diagnosis came after Brandon had complained of several symptoms. Brandon was a freshman at Thomas Worthington High School and played on the football team. During the hot, two-a-day practices held in August, Brandon had passed out on the football field. At first, we didn't think too much of his passing out. After all, it was August and the usual ninety degree temperatures that Ohio summers bring could cause anyone to pass out. But, other symptoms began to present themselves and further testing was followed by the diagnosis.

Brandon spent the next year and a half dealing with treatment for this disease. He had chemotherapy every week. The treatment was a rotation of infusions given at Children's Hospital one week and medication taken daily at home the next week. The infusions made him very sick to his stomach for a few days and also compromised his immune system. Before each infusion Brandon had a blood draw through which they checked his white blood cell count. On several occasions, the white blood cell count was to low and he was unable to continue with infusions that week. Because his immune system was compromised, he was hospitalized often during the treatment period with various infections.

Our family had always been a close family and we remained close during this difficult time in our lives. Our faith that God would bring Brandon through this difficult time was strengthened by the support of our family, friends, church, and community.

Brandon's cancer soon fell into remission, but he continued to receive chemotherapy and deal with the side effects of the treatment throughout his high school years. The support from our community continued as well and we received a multitude of blessings from those who were familiar with our journey. During this time, Bill also had several surgeries to remove cancerous melanoma cells. As we struggled to regain our sense of control over our lives, our priorities began to change.

I received a call from The Special Wish Foundation, a foundation that grants wishes for children with life-threatening illnesses. I was told during this conversation that several people had contacted their organization and had shared with them the story of Brandon's diagnosis and our family's struggle. They had called to offer Brandon "a special wish." Brandon could have wished for anything: a trip to Disney World; to meet a favorite athlete or TV star; or a shopping spree. Brandon's wish was to spend time on a dude ranch out west.

The Special Wish Foundation had been granting wishes for children for many years. One thing they had learned was that the illness of a child affects the entire family, not just the child who has the illness. Often the other children in the family take a back seat to the sick child, who gets a lot of attention. Mom and Dad need to spend a great deal of time at the hospital or doctor visits with the sick child and the other children are left behind with friends and family members. And, of course, Mom and Dad are trying to juggle work commitments along with hospital visits. Therefore, the whole family was invited to join Brandon on his Wish experience to get away from the stress of the illness and enjoy some precious time together.

The Special Wish Foundation flew our family to Tucson, Arizona, where we spent a week at The White Stallion Guest Ranch. The owners and the staff of this ranch went above and beyond to make our stay a memorable one for our entire family. Brandon, Missy, and Shane spent much of their time riding horses, hanging out with the wranglers, and enjoying all that the ranch had to offer. They were out of bed early in the morning so that they could help the wranglers with their chores and they loved every minute of it. Bill and I also enjoyed riding the horses over the beautiful countryside of Tucson. Delicious meals were served both in their comfortable dining room and outdoors at different locations throughout the ranch. Daily activities kept us busy and entertained. We came home refreshed and ready to deal with the next step in our journey.

As our priorities continued to change, our family visited several other guest ranches. During one of our visits, Brandon made the comment to Bill, "Dad, we could do something like this." And, a seed was planted.

Brandon attended The Ohio State University upon graduation from high school. Following his freshman year, he made the decision to transfer to Hocking College in Nelsonville, Ohio. Hocking College is a small, hands on college that offers course work in many alternative career areas. Brandon chose to work toward a degree in Back Country Horsemanship. With his love of horses and the outdoors, he fit right in. The Back Country Horsemanship course work included a wide variety of training and experiences such as: riding and training horses; making and repairing tack; horse shoeing; horse care; team driving; and mapping, among others.

During the summer, Brandon was hired as a wrangler at Whistling Acres Guest Ranch in Colorado. He was able to put to use all the things he had learned during his first year at Hocking College. Brandon thoroughly enjoyed his summer at Whistling Acres. The owners and managers were great people and made him feel like part of the family.

Brandon also worked during the winter quarter at Vista Verde Guest Ranch in Steamboat Springs, Colorado. At this ranch, Brandon cared for the horses, but a big part of his job was driving a team of horses. The horses pulled a sleigh that the guests enjoyed riding through the snow. After completing his course work in the Back Country Horsemanship program, Brandon also worked on a guest ranch in Rifle, Colorado.

While Brandon was busy learning about horses and working on guest ranches, Bill was equally busy researching the guest ranch industry and learning everything he could about the business end of running a guest ranch. Over time, thoughtful discussion and many prayers, Bill and I made the decision to purchase a guest ranch. Bill sought the help of a realtor in Colorado and had begun the search.

The search for a guest ranch didn't come easy either. Over the course of nearly two years, Bill and I (when I was able to go along) looked at countless ranches. Offers to purchase were made on a few ranches, but nothing seemed to come together. We had nearly given up our search, thinking that perhaps this was not the proper time for this venture. We had even started to look closer to home at other opportunities, even the possibility of opening a bed and breakfast. Just before submitting an offer to purchase a bed and breakfast in Ohio, the realtor that Bill was working with gave Bill a call and was excited for us to come to Wyoming to look at a ranch in the Big Horn Mountains.

Ranger Creek Guest Ranch was located just west of Sheridan, Wyoming, and just east of Cody, Wyoming. Bill and I had actually taken a trip to this area when we graduated from high school. One day while we were traveling, we stopped by a creek to soak our feet in the clear mountain stream that ran beside the road. While we were there, Bill had made the comment, "You know, someday I wouldn't mind living out here." Some people may call that a coincidence, we call it God's plan.

As we drove the highway over the mountain from Sheridan, I had the feeling that this just might be the Ranch that we had been looking for. One of the important criteria for me when choosing a ranch was that it be surrounded by green. Living in Ohio all of my life, green grass and green trees were important to me. The

Big Horn Mountains are covered in beautiful lodge pole pines. And, the run off from the winter snows provide miles of green meadows. As we drew closer to the ranch, we turned onto the dirt road that snaked farther up the mountain. We crossed a creek, Shell Creek, with its crystal clear sparkling water. Turning into the lane, we were welcomed by the traditional western cross bar entrance: "Welcome to Ranger Creek Guest Ranch." As we drove through the trees to the point where we could see the Ranch, Bill and I were so excited. The Ranch was exactly what we had been looking for.

Brandon, Bill and I

History of the Ranch

The Ranch is located in the Big Horn National Forest. The National Forest Service owns the ground that the Ranch sits on, but the improvements, the lodge, cabins, shower/laundry facility, outbuildings, and water system are privately owned. The Forest Service manages the permits that allow the use of the ground that the improvements sit on. And, there is a yearly fee for the use of the land. Certain restrictions are placed on the use of the land.

All improvements to the facilities and use of the land must meet the standards of the Forest Service and are subject to their approval or rejection. It is sometimes a costly and lengthy process to gain approval for improvements or changes to the facilities. As is frequently the case, dealing with the government and the "red tape" that is involved can be frustrating and time consuming.

As part of the lease for the Ranch, there is also a "drop camp" located in the wilderness area near Shell Lake. This drop camp provides the opportunity to offer pack trips to those guests that desire to rough it for a few days in the wilderness area. This drop camp is also useful during hunting season. The hunters pack into the drop camp and hunt out of this more remote segment of the forest.

The lease for the area that is now known as Ranger Creek Guest Ranch started in 1918 as a small cabin and tent spike camp. It derived its name from the small

creek that ran through the property. It was owned by
W.H. Wyman & Sons. In 1929, Trapper Lodge, Inc.
purchased the lease. Trapper Lodge, Inc. owned a lodge
at the base of the mountain in Shell and used this property as a spike camp for overnight camping and hunting camps. E.T. Foe purchased the lease in 1934 while
he was logging the timber in the national forest around
the ranch and a few years later built the existing lodge
as his headquarters. A sawmill was set up near the creek
to mill the logs for the lodge from the standing timber
in the forest. The cabins were added a few at a time and
used as housing for his workers.

During World War II, the Ranch was closed. After
the war, Glen and Vera Foe purchased the Ranch from
E.T. Foe, his brother.

From records provided by the Big Horn National
Forest Service the following individuals owned the Ranch:

Year PurchasedOwner

1950D.K. Jones

1961Albert Gillette

1964Chas A. Huffman

1968Louis Middaugh

1969Maurice Carney

1979James Moore

1991Al Powell & Dick Kalasinsky

1998Bill & Sue Comisford

Ken Jones (D.K. Jones) owned the Ranch with his wife for eleven years. He still lived in the area and would join us from time to time for dinner. The stories he told about his days at the Ranch were full of joy and sheer pleasure to hear. His stories always included his wife and the joy on his face shown with the loving memories he held of her and their years on the Ranch. She had passed away several years before we moved to the area and Ken dearly missed her. Ken was nearly blind now, but those memories held for him visions dearer than those seen with perfect eyes.

Jim Moore and his wife dropped by the Ranch often and talked about both the joys and the tribulations of owning the Ranch. Jim told us stories of the terrible devastation the Ranch suffered from a tornado. Many of the cabins were left in ruins and trees were strewn all over the property. Jim brought his children along on one visit to the Ranch. His children were now adults but had grown up on the Ranch. I can remember his daughter walking around the Ranch and you could see the tears welling up in her eyes as the memories rushed through her mind. She was pleasantly surprised as she walked through the horses and recognized a few that still remained from their own string of horses.

Over the years many previous owners, wranglers, and staff members stopped by to visit the Ranch. The love of the Ranch was so apparent on their faces and in their stories. These people came and left the Ranch for many different reasons, but they took with them memories that will last a lifetime.

I never grew weary of meeting these people and hearing their stories. Looking back, I hope that they understood that I could have listened to their stories for hours. Now as I recall my memories of the Ranch I understand the importance of those visits coupled with the heartfelt love for the Ranch that we all share.

GREYBULL, WYOMING   GREYBULL, WYOMING

Brochure of Ranger Creek Ranch during the early 1960's

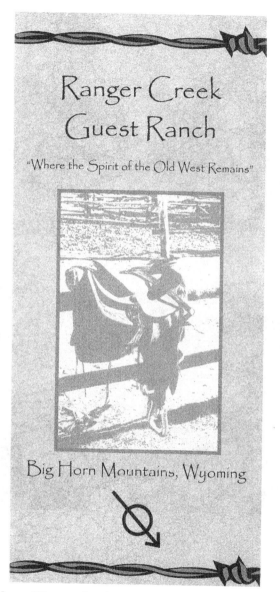

Brochure of Ranger Creek Guest Ranch during our ownership.

Rebuilding of the Ranch

We purchased the Ranch in September and made the decision to spend the month of October at the Ranch to start the renovations and some of the ground work we needed to open for business the next summer. Our son Shane and daughter Missy both lived in apartments while they attended their respective colleges and they remained in Ohio to continue their coursework. Bill, Brandon and I quickly started to work. We began establishing ourselves in the communities of Sheridan, Shell, and Greybull. Depending on what service or item we needed, we would visit one of these towns. We began to understand how much we had taken for granted while living in Ohio. Sheridan was one and a half hours from the Ranch. Shell, a small town at the base of the mountain where we picked up our mail, was half an hour from the Ranch. And, Greybull, (population 1,700) where we purchased most of our groceries, was fifty minutes from the Ranch. We decided that keeping an on-going supply list for anyone who was going off the mountain would become a necessity.

One evening during our stay at the Ranch, we decided to take a break and go for pizza. We drove to Greybull. Greybull reminded us of an old western town like you might see in the movies, only with a few updates. The town had only one street light, which was one of two that were used in the whole county. The people who lived in Greybull and the surrounding area were friendly and as we walked down the street, we were greeted with a friendly smile and a few kind words. That particular night, as we walked into the local pizza shop, it was evident that we were the "new people in town." Everyone became deafly quiet and all eyes were on us as we placed our order. It was definitely an awkward moment, but as time passed, that pizza shop became one of our favorite places to eat and some of those people became our good friends.

Bill and Brandon began work to build a front porch on the lodge. Bill's brother, Randy, and his good friend, Mike, came out to help with the building of the porch. Back in Ohio, I was known for my delicious brownies. Whenever we were visiting friends or family they would say, "Sue, bring some of your brownies." So, I decided to surprise the guys with some one afternoon while they were building the front porch. While preparing meals for the guys, I was learning that cooking and particularly baking at an altitude of 8300 feet was a challenge. At high elevations, the boiling point for water is lower because there is decreased air pressure. Boxed cake mix back in Ohio had suggestions for cooking at higher elevations, starting at 3,000 feet, but I wasn't sure how the altitude at the Ranch would affect the brownies. I decided to start with no changes to the recipe and see what happened. Although the first batch of brownies looked soft and chewy when they came out of the oven, when I attempted to cut them, they were as hard as rock. Determined to bake suitable brownies, I started over and this time I adjusted the ingredients, adding more flour and less oil. I also decreased the baking temperature slightly. This time they came out of the oven soft and chewy. I immediately cut the brownies and carried them to the guys on the front porch. They ate the brownies and told me how good they were. Later that evening after dinner, I brought the remaining brownies to the table to serve them and as I attempted to cut them, I realized that once again they were hard as rock. Although the guys teased me about the brownies, I think they were a little nervous even commenting that the brownies would need to be surgically removed from their bellies. They claim to this day that the batch of brownies is holding up the corner of the front porch. I eventually found the right combination of flour, oil and baking temperature to create delicious brownies, cakes and cookies.

Bill and I quickly learned that the people in the town of Greybull were friendly and that agreements were made with a handshake. Bill had stopped in the local Coop Building Center in Greybull to talk to them about some supplies that were needed to begin the construction in the cabins when we returned in the spring. He knew that those supplies would need to be delivered now while the road to the Ranch was still passable. When he walked in to the building center, he introduced himself as the new owner of Ranger Creek Guest Ranch and explained what supplies he needed. Scott was super friendly and enthusiastic about helping Bill complete a list of supplies and was also interested to hear about the improvements that were contemplated for the Ranch. Scott asked Bill if he was interested in setting up an account, to which Bill agreed.

As Bill started to head for the door, he turned and asked Scott, "Do you need my name?"

Scott smiled and said, "Yea, we should probably write that down."

Much was accomplished during the month of October. The front porch was complete, work was started on the water lines to the cabins, we had made needed contacts, and laid the groundwork for our return in the spring. We left the Ranch and returned to Ohio for the winter.

Bill continued to work on plans for the Ranch. He developed a brochure and website, continued developing contacts within the tourist industry, and attended travel shows as an avenue to attract guests. I began tackling the problem of the telephone system.

The telephone system at the Ranch was an antiquated system similar in concept to the old switchboard system. When someone called the Ranch, it would ring into a system in Sheridan and they would transfer the call to the lodge. It was difficult to get through, not private, and would only stay connected for a very short time. There were no telephone lines across the mountain, so a normal system was not an option. Cellular connection was also not a possibility as there were no towers close enough to pick up a signal. I was determined to find a solution for this problem. After seeing a program on television speaking to this same issue, I began researching the possibility of having telephone lines installed across the mountain. Since there were other businesses on the mountain, I thought maybe they would be interested in the service also.

Through my research, I learned who owned the access rights to the telephone service on the mountain. After several telephone calls and transfers to several different people, I eventually spoke to a very knowledgeable man who seemed to have the answer. George explained to me that in order for him to determine the cost involved in having telephone lines installed on the mountain, I would first need to call the telephone company and place an order. Following his instructions, I placed an order for a telephone at the Ranch. Now, I will remind you that we are back in Ohio, the Ranch is closed, no one is there, and there is about 200 inches of snow on the ground at the Ranch. Our nearest neighbor in the winter is at least ten miles away. The following week I receive a telephone call from the telephone company. The *young girl* on the other end of the phone explains to me that she needs to set up an appointment for someone to come to the Ranch and install our telephone. I proceed to explain to her that the Ranch is closed; no one is there and it is in the middle of nowhere. I also explain that this is just a process that needs to be followed in order to ascertain the cost of installing lines across the mountain. There is a slight pause followed by, "Okay, so...will you be home (at the ranch) between 11:00 a.m. and 1:00 p.m. on Wednesday?" Once again, I explain that George is just trying to ascertain the cost of installing lines and that no actual phone needs to be installed at this time, etc., etc. And, again I hear, "Okay, so... will you be home between 11:00 a.m. and 1:00 p.m. on Wednesday?" This time I just answer, "Yes."

A few weeks later, I receive the highly anticipated call from George. He states that he has good news. He proceeds to tell me that the telephone company is willing to install telephone lines across the mountain. Then he explains that all I need to do is find ten people (or businesses) on the mountain to contribute $100,000.00 each and we can have telephone lines. After thanking him for all his efforts, I tell him that since I have not even met many of the people who own businesses on the mountain that I may find it hard asking them for $100,000.00. I could just see it, "Hi, I'm Sue, one of the new owners of Ranger Creek Guest Ranch. Do you have $100,000.00 that you would like to contribute to installing telephone lines?" I decided to look at other alternatives.

During our stay in Sheridan when we originally came to look at the Ranch, I remembered seeing an advertisement from a local cell phone company. The advertisement featured a cowboy sitting on his horse while riding across the mountain. He was talking on his cell phone. I had written down the name of the cellular company, so I decided to give them a call. When I inquired about service at the Ranch with their company, they said that they could not provide cellular service up on the mountain. Puzzled by this, I explained to him that I had seen the advertisement of a cowboy talking on his cell phone while riding his horse across the mountain. The gentlemen sheepishly replied, "Oh, yeah that is a nice advertisement, but we really can't do that."

The problem with the telephone system continued and during the winter of 1999 Brandon and Bill drove snowmobiles back and forth across the mountain that lay behind the Ranch with an antenna in hand trying to locate a strong cell signal. Finally they were able to locate a signal at the top of the ridge in the horse pasture and up the mountain from the paddock area. They marked the spot with a T post which disappeared in the deep snow. Once the snow had melted and the ground was accessible again, Bill and Brandon installed a small cell system at the top of the hill and laid cable down to the lodge. The system was not perfect, but much better than what we started with. There were times when we still could not get a signal at the Ranch but we had learned that a few miles up the mountain, across from Snowshoe Lodge; we were able to find a signal. We called this location "the phone booth" and used it often.

We also installed a satellite dish in order to gain access to the internet and booked most of our reservations through that system. Satellite systems where not commonly used in that area which explained our customer number of 1515. Internet access was extremely fast because there were so few people using the system.

Our plans were to permanently move to the Ranch in mid-April. As the time drew near, we were busy making all the necessary arrangements. Our daughter, Missy, was attending college at Columbus State, a small community college, and Shane was in his sophomore year at The Ohio State University. They were staying in Ohio to finish college. The most difficult part of leaving Ohio was leaving without them. Even though I knew that they had their friends and our families close by to support them, I felt as though I was abandoning them.

Of course they had the option of coming with us, but they needed to stay in Ohio and finish college. We were always a close family and leaving them behind made me feel very sad.

Following months of preparation, tearful goodbyes, along with exciting expectations, moving day finally arrived. Bill, Brandon and I, along with Kayleen and Peanut, departed Ohio to begin our journey to Ranger Creek Guest Ranch in Wyoming.

Mike (Peanut) and Kayleen had attended Hocking College with Brandon and we had hired them to work for us at the Ranch. They had agreed to help with the construction, repair, and cleanup and then work as wranglers once we officially opened for business.

Our caravan across 1,800 miles included our Suburban pulling a trailer, a moving van, and Peanut and Kayleen's truck. Our dog, Cali, Brandon's dog, Layla, and Peanut and Kayleen's dog, Kasha, were along for the ride. On the third day, we arrived in Sheridan, Wyoming. We unloaded the moving van and the trailer into storage units, picked up some groceries, two snow-mobiles, and headed up the mountain to the Ranch.

We had been well informed that the winters in the Big Horn Mountains lasted long after the snow was gone in Ohio. Our plans had been made accordingly and that was a deciding factor in postponing our move to the Ranch until mid-April. I don't know if it was naiveté or just wishful thinking, but since it was sixty degrees in Sheridan and there was no sign of snow, I was sure that we wouldn't need the snowmobiles.

As we started up the mountain, I felt so assured that I was right and that we would be able to drive right into the Ranch. All those months of worrying about the snow were so wasteful. A few miles further up the mountain it started flurrying. No need to worry, we can deal with a few flurries. A little farther up the mountain, we passed a snow plow. Wow, they even come out for a few flurries. I soon learned that the higher the elevation the deeper the snow. By the time we crested the high point of the mountain, we could hardly see as the snow was falling so hard. The snow on top of the mountain was well over my head. The drive across the mountain was beautiful and looked like a winter wonderland. Snowmobiles were everywhere as the snowmobilers played in the deep and abundant snow. The road crews had crafted large rows of mounded snow which they used as wind breaks on the flat part of the mountain to shield the road from drifting.

As we drove across the mountain, we started smelling this sweet, grape smell. We had brought along a bottle of wine to celebrate the occasion. I had stuck the bottle underneath my seat in the Suburban. In my haste to leave the motel room, I neglected to put my nightgown in my suitcase, so I also quickly stuck it beneath my seat. Suddenly it occurred to me what had happened. The cork in the wine bottle had popped in the high altitude. Fortunately my nightgown absorbed most of the wine and left little stain on the carpet of the Suburban.

After turning onto Paintrock Road, we were only able to drive about a mile on the dirt road into the Ranch. We parked the trucks, unloaded the snowmobiles, and began the three mile trek into the Ranch.

The lodge had sat empty from shortly after we had left in October until now and it was *cold*. The temperature outside was five degrees below zero and probably not much warmer on the inside. After quickly starting a fire, we went to bed. We all had blankets piled so high on each of our beds that we could hardly move. It took about twenty-four hours for the lodge to heat up, but once it was heated, it was nice and cozy.

The first few weeks posed several challenges. There were problems with the water system. When the excavator and plumber had worked at the Ranch in October, they had uncovered and severed a water line. Instead of repairing it, they covered it up. Bill discovered that the broken line was the line that carried water into the lodge. Since the line could not be repaired until the weather permitted (early June), we had to carry water from the shower house to the lodge to cook and do dishes. But, the water lines into the shower house were frozen and had to be unthawed. Until the lines were thawed, it was melted snow water that was used to prepare meals and bathe.

Bill's mother and father (Bill and Jo) decided that they were going to surprise us and drove from Ohio to pay us a visit. They thought, as I did, that they would be able to drive right into the Ranch. Upon discovering our trucks parked along the road, they had to drive down the mountain to call us and ask us to come and get them on the snowmobiles. Jo's first words after seeing our remote location were, *"Are you nuts?"*

Unlike Ohio, winter seemed to continue well into the spring months which caused a few unexpected problems driving into the Ranch. Although we continued to get a few inches of snow now and then, the accumulated snow was starting to melt. Parts of the road that the sun reached were now bare but the snow was still deep in other spots shaded by the trees. Even though we still could not drive into the Ranch there was not enough snow to run the snowmobiles. We had to walk the mile between the Ranch and the bottom of the hill. Carrying groceries and construction supplies up the hill was difficult. Brandon and Peanut carried drywall mud on a pole balanced between them up the steep road and into the Ranch.

Finally, the weekend before Memorial Day, we were able to have the road plowed so we could drive into the Ranch. We all celebrated as the snowplow plowed its way into the Ranch. We decided to take a few hours off and went to Greybull for pizza.

The five of us, and now Bill and Jo, worked very hard during those first two months. We literally worked from sun up to sun down. There was no television at the Ranch. But, that was okay, because we didn't have time to watch it anyway. The guys constructed bathrooms in the cabins which meant removing the heavy cast iron stoves that were in the middle of each cabin. The next step was constructing walls and rough plumbing the shower stalls, sinks, and toilets in preparation for the plumber to finish installing the plumbing. New heating systems were also installed in each cabin.

Kayleen, Jo, and I cleaned everything in the lodge and in the cabins: walls, windows, and furniture. The wool blankets in the cabins were very warm, but they all needed to be washed and mended. We sorted through the sheets determining which ones could be used and which ones to throw away. I made new curtains for all the cabins and mended all the blankets. The cabinets in the kitchen were sanded down and painted and the floors in the lodge and the cabins were sanded and sealed.

Over the previous three years while we explored guest ranches to purchase, I had picked up, at various locations including flea markets, antique stores, and western stores, items to decorate the cabins. I kept a file with pages pulled from magazines with ideas for decorating. I watched for sales on quilts, throw rugs, and fabric that I could use to decorate incorporating a western theme. Decorating the cabins was certainly enjoyable for me. Along with the antique beds several of the cabins also came with log beds. Using antiques that we brought along from Ohio and the western items that I had accumulated, the cabins presented a western character that was welcoming and fun for the guests. A few of the cabins already had wooden plaques displaying their names and with Shane's help, we added a few of our own. The guest cabins were named: Aspen, Custer, Buffalo Bill, Shoshone, and Bridger.

Previously, the Ranch had a shower house that was used by the staff and the guests. There was an appointed girls' side and a boys' side. Since we were installing bathrooms in each separate cabin, we adapted one side of the shower house as a laundry room. We installed two washers and two dryers and a long folding table.

This not only insured additional room in the lodge, where the laundry had previously been located, but also provided much needed storage space for storing bedding, towels, guest soaps, and other stock items. The other side of the shower house remained for the use of the staff.

Once the weather broke, we moved to the outside and began painting the buildings and constructing and repairing fence. Several other family members and friends came out to help wherever they could lend a hand.

Brandon and Peanut were given jack hammers to bore through the slabs of granite under the cabins to make room for the water and sewer lines for the new bathrooms. Once the construction was finished in the cabins, the plumber took over and installed the water and sewer lines. Part of the construction was a 120' x 80' leach bed that lay in the front pasture. It was quit an impressive hole in the ground that could be seen from the steep mountain road above the Ranch. We were told later that the rumor had been spread that Ranger Creek was putting in a massive swimming pool. Even though we lived in a remote location, we were becoming part of the community and talk of the changes we were making to one of its historical and treasured landmarks was big news in the nearby towns of Shell and Greybull. Many of the local residents stopped by to see what changes we were making and seemed happy with the renovations and our future plans for the Ranch. The locals were genuinely friendly people who often stopped us during our trips to town to pick up supplies to ask about our progress and talk about their fondness for Ranger Creek.

Although we still had much to accomplish, in two months' time, Bill and I, along with Brandon, Peanut and Kayleen, family members, and friends had accomplished so much. Our goals were overwhelming but our progress steady and sure. As our first guests drove up the driveway, the plumber was flushing the toilet in their cabin for the first time. Our joy was evident and our dream was truly beginning. Ranger Creek Guest Ranch was once again open and ready to serve the public in the style and greatness that it so richly deserved.

Horses

Seven horses were part of the assets purchased with the Ranch:

Shebah was an old Palomino mare, swayback and thin. She had seen better days.

Gizzy was a small, stout Palomino mare. Gizzy reminded one of a carousel horse, with her beautiful white mane and tail and her blond coloring. Her feisty attitude made her fun to watch.

Molly was an Appaloosa mare, grey in color. Although she had lost sight in one eye, she remained the leader of the herd and became my favorite of all the horses.

Cinnamon was a beautiful, big sorrel mare. Her name fit her well as her color was the color of cinnamon. Cinnamon was very well behaved for women and children riders, but often misbehaved when ridden by adult men.

Ginger, a chestnut mare had a beautiful grayish mane.

Ringo, a smaller brown horse, possessed the most character of all the horses. He was a lady's man and always aligned himself with one of the mares. Known for his heavy coat of hair, Ringo was also known for his ability to escape through fences. Although he never wandered far from the Ranch he always made his way back to the pasture well before feeding time. Ringo was often the first to greet guests in the morning by peering through the cabin windows.

Baldy, a tall, quarter horse paint with a white face was the youngest of the herd. Baldy had been trained and used to herd cattle and was definitely the most spirited of the herd. He was rather bored with trail rides, but when given the opportunity to wrangle cattle, he perked right up and took the lead.

Horses are herd animals. They tend to be loyal and protective of those in their own herd. They often surprised me at the emotion they showed when one of their own was taken away or hurt. Since Shebah was getting older and no longer able to withstand the physical pressure of carrying a person during a trail ride, we decided to sell her to a nearby ranch. The day Bill and Brandon drove Shebah off the Ranch, Gizzy followed the horse trailer through the pasture as far as she could go whinnying along the way. And, when it came time to sell Gizzy and Ginger, Ringo stood beside the empty trailer upon its return for several days. He wouldn't eat and stood with his head low to the ground mourning their absence. It was heart breaking.

Later in the summer we added *Seminol* (Semi for short) to our herd of horses. Semi was an adopted horse as part of the wild mustang roundup. She was a beautiful Sorrel mare with a long, blond mane. Introducing Semi into the herd was comical. She was kept in a separate paddock for a week and slowly introduced to the other horses. She was finally permitted in the pasture with the other horses. Baldy, with the other horses close behind, appeared serious with their ears laid back as they confronted Semi. She spun and kicked at every horse in sight. Semi was letting them know that she was at the top of the pecking order where she remained until she left the Ranch.

A few years later I purchased Sadie at a horse auction in Basin. Sadie is a tall horse, standing at 15-2 hands, buckskin in color. She has a beautiful dark brown mane and four dark brown socks. When we purchased Sadie, we were told that she was with foal. A few months later, we had our vet draw blood from Sadie and had it checked. The blood test came back negative.

Early in the spring, just after returning from Ohio, we stopped by our property in Shell to check on the horses and were pleasantly surprised when we saw Sadie. She was definitely with foal and big as a barn. Sadie was due to deliver in early June and everyone at the Ranch was eager to see the new foal. A few of the wranglers slept down near the paddock area in case she delivered in the middle of the night. But early one morning, Bill came running up to the lodge to tell me that Sadie had delivered the foal.

Cheyenne was the cutest little thing and it was amazing to watch as he clumsily learned how to use his spindly legs only minutes after his birth. Cheyenne was full of spirit and quickly learned how to buck and kick up his legs. It was fun to watch him as he ran around the pasture kicking up his heels along the way. He was so ornery and would back into Sadie pushing her back away from the hay. Sadie was protective of him, but ignored his little antics.

Although he loved to be handled and loved for me to brush him and rub his ears, when Bill had to give him a shot, even with several of the wranglers holding him down, he managed to jerk away, hitting Bill in the head and knocking Bill out for few minutes.

Along with the ten to twelve horses that we owned, we also leased around thirty head of horses during the summer season. This number of horses was needed in order to accommodate the number of guests that vacationed with us in a given week and also to have a good mix of horses for the different riding levels of our guests. A beginner rider could not be put on a horse that should only be ridden by an advanced rider just as an advanced rider might be bored on a slow paced horse that plodded along. We leased horses through a few different companies, but for the most part used an outfit out of Pavilion, Wyoming. This company was a family owned company that had leased horses to ranches in Wyoming and Montana for many years. They knew their business well and had passed the business down through several generations of the family. The daughter, a tall, gorgeous tomboy, had learned to work well with their clientele and was our contact while we leased horses from them.

Early in the spring each guest ranch would make a trip to Pavilion to choose a string of horses for the upcoming season. Choosing horses was usually a day long event. Pavilion was a three hour drive from the Ranch, through the Wind River Canyon. After a hearty lunch served by the Pavilion group, the task of choosing horses sometimes took another couple of hours. As we became familiar with the horses, we could choose to keep horses from the previous season. This enabled us to build a consistent string of horses that we were comfortable with. Those early years of riding and selecting horses provided a few stories that were told and retold. The Pavilion group thoroughly enjoyed this time of year and was good at setting riders up for "a rodeo" at times. Their favorite saying was, "This is the best horse we have." Truth be known, the horse might have only been ridden a few times.

It was common to see a horse come unglued during this trial riding period. And when one horse comes unglued, oftentimes the others follow suit. I particularly remember one story when the owner's paperwork went flying out of her hand from a gust of wind which caused several horses to spook and sent riders flying.

Once the horses were selected, the Pavilion group would deliver horses and tack to the Ranch once the snow had disappeared. Our horses were delivered at a drop-off point near the Ranch. Delivery day was always an exciting day for the wranglers. It was their first look at the horses they would be riding for the season. Depending on the experience of the wranglers, the horses were either ridden (while leading another horse) up the road to the Ranch or "run" up the road to the Ranch. It was an awesome sight to watch twenty to thirty horses running the mountain road.

Delivery day was a busy day on the Ranch. After gathering the horses in the paddock area, each horse had to be wormed. A notebook, with a section for each horse was kept with information such as, delivery dates, dates they were wormed, injuries (cuts or scrapes), and any treatment they received. The saddles, blankets, and bridles were sorted, cleaned, and labeled according to the horses they would be used on. Bill and the wranglers then rode each horse to determine the ranking of the horse. The ranking coincided with riding abilities of the guests. A spirited horse may be given a ranking of wrangler or advanced rider only. While an easy going horse would be ranked children's horse or beginner rider. Notes were kept on the horses throughout the season.

Bill and the wranglers were consistent about matching the rider with the proper horse, which allowed the guests to feel more comfortable on the trail rides. The guests were matched with a horse more closely resembling their riding ability and nature. Bill's favorite saying, which was heard often in the guest ranch industry, is, "We have gentle horses for gentle people; we have spirited horses for spirited people; and for those people who don't like to ride, we have horses that don't like to be ridden."

The first few years while building our summer business, we were busy with hourly trail rides. Tourists driving across the mountain or staying at the Lodge Loop at Burgess Junction would drop by the Ranch to participate in hourly trail rides. We offered an hour, two hour, and half day ride with lunch. This gave us another opportunity to market the Ranch and show off the improvements we had made to the facilities. As was the intention, many of these riders booked future vacations as a result of the enjoyment they experienced during their trail ride. We looked forward to seeing many of the hourly trail riders back several years in a row until we became so busy with week-long reservations that we no longer were able to accommodate the hourly trail rides.

Since the hourly trail riders dropped by at any time of the day, the wranglers had to drop what they were doing and saddle the horses on a minute's notice. I enjoyed talking with the riders and showing them around the Ranch while the wranglers prepared their horses. On one occasion, I recognized the two riders as an actor and actress on a daytime soap opera that I watched while back in Ohio. On another occasion, Gary Anderson, the kicker for one of the pro-football teams stopped by with his family to enjoy a trail ride. It was always fun to talk with people and hear where they were from and learn about their family.

Our first summer season during a trail ride, one of the gals lost her wallet somewhere along the ride. Although the wranglers searched for the wallet along the trail, it was nowhere to be found. We took the riders information just in case it was found later. Much to our amazement, an entire year had passed by when one day, during a trail ride, the wrangler spied the wallet laying alongside the trail. We were able to return the wallet intact back to its owner.

Brandon packed a group from the Geological Survey Team into the Wilderness Area to conduct a study on the fish habitat. When the guys arrived, a few of them were wearing shorts and sandals. Although Bill and Brandon cautioned them that they might not be comfortable riding in shorts and sandals especially since they would be riding through overgrown areas, they insisted they would be fine. Brandon had to limit them on the amount of equipment that could be handled by the two pack horses chosen for the trip. The guys were troopers and completed their assigned survey within a few days. Even the shorts and sandals withstood the trek through the wilderness and although it was a work trip, they commented how much they enjoyed their horseback ride and the remarkable scenery along the way.

My husband, Bill and Billy the wrangler were hired to try to find a horse that had gotten loose during an endurance race that took place in the foothills just above Shell. The race took place in early August and the weather was hot and dry at the base of the mountain causing concern that the horse would not have sufficient water. When last seen, the horse was still wearing its saddle and bridle which caused additional concern for fear the bridle and saddle would become tangled with brush or overgrowth in the area.

Bill and Billy spent the entire day combing the area, which was steep and laden with rock. This area is also rattlesnake territory. Although Bill and Billy were unable to locate the horse before nightfall, the horse was located a few days later with the assistance of a local helicopter. The horse was dehydrated but otherwise unharmed.

Bill's horse Duke seemed to enjoy playing with the wranglers on occasion. During a trail ride Jeff, a wrangler, got down to close the gate leaving Duke to graze. Duke teased Jeff by staying just far enough in front of him to avoid Jeff reaching his reins and leading Jeff in a figure eight for a few minutes before stopping to allow Jeff to climb back on him. Our son Shane had ridden Duke up to the spring located 1,350 feet up the mountain behind the lodge. Duke decided not to stick around and took off running back to the paddock as soon as Shane dismounted and let loose of his reins.

Jeff was riding Gizzy bareback one evening as the wranglers returned to the Ranch after an evening ride. As Jeff passed in front of the lodge, he waved to Bill and me on the front porch. As Jeff tipped his hat with his right hand to wave, he slid right off of Gizzy. Jeff jumped up grabbing his hat and sheepishly glanced toward the porch to see if anyone had noticed him falling.

Bill and the wranglers loved to ride the horses and on occasion race on the roads up above Crooked Creek

Canyon. As Bill, and the wranglers, Billy, John, and Nikki started racing, Bill and Billy quickly passed John with John acknowledging his retreat by saying, "Hi Billy! Bye Billy!" Nikki's horse could not keep up and as herd animals often do, he started to whinny as a signal to his fellow horses that he was left behind. As Bill and Billy turned the corner and crested the hill a truck pulling a horse trailer appeared on the road in front of them. Without hesitation Bill and Billy continued with their race parting ways only for the truck and trailer and meeting up on the road once again. Bill claims that he won this race, but if you talk to Billy he may have a different story.

Many of the wranglers had their favorite horses that they rode year after year. Tanya loved C.O.D. and cried when she had to take him back at the end of the season. Shane enjoyed working with Arapahoe. Arapahoe was a beautiful, quarter horse paint. He was a young horse when he first came to the Ranch and Shane worked with him throughout the summer gaining his confidence and training him to ride. Bubba was a big, black horse and had extra-large lips. Shane provided entertainment by making Bubba mouth the words, "You ain't nothing but a hound dog." Billy's favorite was Stanley.

The paddock area was a busy place in the morning as the wranglers brushed and saddled the horses. Horses were lined up side by side as the wranglers prepared them for their trail ride. Chipmunks were plentiful and fearlessly ran around the paddock area and tack room. Our dog, Lucy, enjoyed chasing the chipmunks. One morning as the wranglers were saddling the horses,

Lucy chased a chipmunk underneath the bellies of eight horses with the chipmunk running up the leg of the last horse to escape Lucy's pursuit. The horses all remained unconcerned as the game of chase took place beneath them.

As the summer season ended and the fall season began, the leased horses would be returned to the Pavilion group in stages. Returning the horses down the mountain road usually took the better part of a day. Most of our staff had left by this time leaving only two or three of us to return the horses and the saddles to the drop off point. Bill and the other wranglers would lead the horses down the four-mile road to the waiting trailer. My job was to drive the truck, packed with the saddles, blankets, and tack.

I remember well one fall day as we returned the horses, Bill and Tanja had the job of leading the horses down the road. The only truck that was available that day to haul the saddles was the big blue truck. The big blue truck was a flatbed Ford that had a stick shift. We used the blue truck for hauling hay, feeding the horses hay in the pasture, and hauling trash. Since it was a stick shift, it became the learning tool for a few of the wranglers to learn how to drive. I, too, was not comfortable driving a stick shift. This particular day, however, I had no choice.

As I followed Bill and Tanja down the road, I kept the blue truck in the same gear. As we climbed up a hill and drew close to a curve, I could see another vehicle coming toward us. In order to allow the other vehicle to pass by us safely, I had to completely stop the truck.

Every time I tried to start moving again, the truck would coast backwards. Finally, I killed the engine. After several failed attempts at starting the engine, I had coasted to the edge of the road and there was no room left. Beyond the edge of the road was a drop off straight down to the bottom of the canyon. As I tried one last time to start the engine, I said a little prayer: "Please Lord, help me start this truck; it's now or never." The truck started right up and I soon caught up with Bill and Tanja.

Whenever we see past guests they always try to remember the name of the horse that they rode during their stay at the Ranch. Listed below are the names of horses that we leased while at the Ranch.

Ace	Chiko
Antonio	Coco
Apple	Easy
Arapahoe	Fox
Arkansas	Fudge
Banjo	Girappaloosa
Barbelle	Holland
Biscuit	Ivy
Boomer	Jeremiah
Breeze	Jockey
Bubba	Jupiter
Bud	Lazy
Budweiser	Leonard
Bummer	Lucky
C.O.D.	Montreal
Cascade	Mustard
Casper	Norway

Pringles
Ricky
Rocky
Saskatoon
Sheridan
Smokey
Splash
Standard
Stanley
Superior
Swede
Taxi
Terrell
Thurston
Timmy
Tinker

Top
Top Gun
Valentine
Washakie
Windmill

Staffing of the Ranch

A great source of advertising for dude ranches in general is the Dude Ranch Association. In order to join the Dude Ranch Association, a ranch must meet a list of criteria along with submitting an application followed by a lengthy interview with the Board of the Dude Ranch Association. During our interview process, two of the questions that were asked were, "What is the best thing about owning a Dude Ranch?" and, "What is the worst thing about owning a Dude Ranch?" Bill and I decided that the answer to both of these questions is "staffing." We learned that the staff could make a summer season fun or they could make it challenging.

Our staffing needs for the Ranch were a cook, kitchen/cleaning help, and three or four wranglers. The staff were generally young adults who were either still in college or had just completed college. Although we received as many as eighty resumes for these summer positions, the interview process usually took place over the telephone. It is sometimes difficult to judge personalities and job skills over the phone. Although a wrangler position needed specific skills and a high degree of comfort with horses, the most desired asset for all of our staff was "people skills." We were in the entertainment business and it was imperative that the staff is willing and able to get along with and interact with our guests.

Due in part to the remote location of our Ranch, the staff lived there during the summer season. Most of their activities revolved around the Ranch activities and the staff became part of the family. We relied heavily on each other and in the process had a lot of fun times and memorable experiences.

There were few instances when staffing became more of a burden than a joy. The cook position was one of those instances. It seemed that in the first few years we were destined to operate without a cook, leaving that duty up to me. Although we received several resumes for the cook position, they were either asking far more money than we were willing to pay or we didn't feel comfortable with them living among our young staff.

One young man who lived in a nearby town had applied for the position. Bill and I drove to Greybull and sat down and talked with him at length about the position. He seemed like he would fit the position well. Following the interview, we walked across the street and talked to one of his previous employers whom he had listed as a reference on his application. The restaurant owner told us, "He is a great cook, but he will steal you blind if you don't watch him." We decided to continue our search.

I took on the job of cook with apprehension. When Bill and I first talked about buying a ranch, I told him I was willing to do anything but cook. When it was clear that I had no choice in the matter, my usual can-do attitude took over. Since I had come from a large family and my mom was a magnificent cook, I relied on my experiences growing up and learned that I had absorbed more knowledge in the area of cooking than I had ever imagined.

Even though I scoured cook books for recipes, I quickly learned that what the guests really expected was good home-cooked, meat and potato type of meals. The staff and guests alike provided me with their favorite recipes and along with the recipes that I had grown up with, I had a good start. And, although the elevation created a few problems early on, I quickly learned how to adapt the recipes to allow for the high elevation. Homemade rolls and bread were always a staple along with homemade pies and desserts. Bill's grandmother always served homemade jams and jellies with her meals, which I adopted as well. In addition to meals, a bowl of fresh fruit, cold lemonade and ice tea, and warm, freshly baked cookies were awaiting the guests upon their return to the Ranch after a long trail ride.

Cooking was a full time job and required considerable forethought and planning. Considering our remote location and the inability to find a wholesale grocery service that would agree to deliver to the Ranch, it was mandatory that I plan meals a week ahead and keep a well-stocked pantry to ensure that ingredients were available when I needed them. We relied heavily upon the small grocery store in Greybull to order meat and cheese in bulk whenever they could. We would order a rack of ribs, steaks, and pork tenderloins, leaving Bill to cut the meat according to our needs.

Keeping ingredients on hand was possibly the biggest challenge for me as I was so accustom to having a grocery store so close while living in Ohio, that I often would send someone to the store two or three times during the preparation of a large meal. An ongoing grocery list became essential at the Ranch.

I found that I could create a two week menu and rotate that same menu throughout the summer season. Although I would substitute different meals occasionally, only the staff knew that the menu was the same, as the guest's normal stay was usually a week to ten days. Throughout the week, we also included a breakfast ride, a lunch ride, and a campfire dinner. Occasionally, the guests wished to spend an overnight outside and meals were served at the campsite. All of these meals required special preparation and logistical planning.

Bill and I also enlisted the services of a friend from Sheridan to come up to the Ranch on occasion and prepare meals. Joel was a wonderful cook and enjoyed Dutch oven cooking. Joel was especially helpful and easy to work with and could be counted on when we had big groups staying at the Ranch.

Most meals served in the lodge were served either buffet or family style. Bill always began the meal with a prayer. He would ask for blessings over the guests and the food and would always end the prayer with, "Bless a safe day and a pretty day on the mountain. Amen."

First Summer Season

Brandon was our first right hand man at the Ranch and was invaluable in helping Bill and me get the Ranch up and running. His education in the Back Country Horsemanship program was a tremendous asset and the knowledge that he had gained from working on other guest ranches contributed greatly to the Ranch's success.

Brandon assisted with the construction of the bathrooms in the cabins, fix up and cleanup of the Ranch, and he was our Head Wrangler the first two years. Singing and playing the guitar around the campfire was another gift Brandon brought to the Ranch. His love of horses, laid back, easy going attitude, and fun loving spirit made him fit right into the Ranch life. The fact that Brandon was in his early twenties, and made a handsome cowboy wearing his Stetson and blue jeans, left many female guests (young and old) carrying a crush as they departed the Ranch for home.

Peanut and Kayleen were a couple who both grew up in Ohio and had attended Hocking College with Brandon. They traveled with us to the Ranch in April 1999 and worked alongside us during the construction and cleanup of the Ranch. As we opened our first summer season, they were wranglers alongside Brandon as well. Brandon, Peanut, and Kayleen worked well together and worked extremely hard.

Kayleen was a cute, petite blond who loved to ride horses and loved to dance. Peanut, who acquired his nickname while at Hocking College, was short in stature but tall in confidence. Peanut also loved horses, loved to dance and could sing and play guitar with the best of them.

We learned quickly that Peanut was accident prone. One day, while Kayleen and I were painting the logs on the front porch, we heard Peanut yell out in pain as he and Brandon were moving something in the storage shed. He had dropped whatever they were moving on his foot. Once Kayleen was assured that he was not seriously hurt, she quietly stated, "I sure do love that guy, but I sure am going to buy a large life insurance policy on him before we get married."

Peanut's ability to find an accident proved particularly worrisome to me during the first experience of running the leased horses up the mountain. I have always been aware of my intuition, but don't always heed the warning it often gives me. On this day, as I sat and watched the new batch of horses as they were unloaded from the horse trailer, one particular horse caused me great concern. It seemed very agitated and spooked. Of course, this was the same horse that Peanut chose to ride up the mountain road. I drove the Suburban, loaded with the saddles and tack, up to the Ranch ahead of the horses and waited, with camera in hand, for the arrival of the herd of horses. As time passed and there was no sign of the wranglers or the horses, I became increasingly concerned. As I sat and watched for what seemed like an hour, I noticed someone walking up the lane and something just didn't seem right. I drove the Suburban down the lane and found Peanut walking up the lane dragging his saddle. Nothing appeared to be broken, but he definitely was confused. When I asked him where everyone else was and what had happened, he did not seem to know. He didn't remember riding a horse or what had taken place earlier that day. He kept asking me over and over where Kayleen was. When I reminded him that they had been riding the horses up the mountain, all he would say was, "No s__t?" And then he would ask again, "What happened?" followed again by, "No s__t?"

As I kept a constant eye on Peanut, soon Bill, Brandon, Kayleen, and the herd of horses appeared through the clearing in the trees. Once the horses were properly attended, I was told that Peanut's horse (the horse that caused me concern) had bucked Peanut off in the middle of the road and he had landed on his head. Although he wouldn't let us take him to the hospital, we kept a close watch over him. After a few days of rest, Peanut was back to his ornery self and ready to resume his normal duties.

Peanut and Kayleen were good, common sense, everyday people who gave so much of themselves during their stay at the Ranch. We learned a lot from them and have fun memories of their time at the Ranch.

Shane, our youngest son, also worked for us that first summer season. Shane could always be counted on to do whatever needed to be done, whether it be construction or riding as a wrangler. Shane really loved the Ranch and especially loved sharing the Ranch with his friends back in Ohio. Every year a group of his friends would come out for a week to ride horses and enjoy the Ranch. They helped out with chores or whatever we asked them to do and we always loved having them come to visit.

Second Summer Season 2000

Jessica (Jess) was hired as a wrangler by Bill and Brandon our second summer season. She had just graduated from college and wanted to work as a wrangler for the summer before starting her career as a teacher. She was from Virginia and one only needed to look at her picture to see why Brandon wanted to hire her. She was a beautiful girl with long brown hair, big brown eyes, and a great big smile that complimented her southern charm. Jess came early in the season and she and Brandon quickly hit it off, working together with the horses, building fences, and painting cabins.

Our son, Shane, and his good friend, Jeff, arrived and our second summer season began. Shane worked as a wrangler with Brandon and Jess. Jeff worked in the kitchen. Jeff was not a morning person and preparing breakfast with Jeff was sometimes comical. Jeff manned the waffle iron with special intensity. Although not missing a beat, he pulled a chair up next to the waffle iron and napped between clicks that awakened him long enough to remove the waffle and add additional batter.

Tanja, was from Germany. She found our Ranch online and Bill immediately enjoyed her chattiness as they emailed back and forth nailing down the details of her employment. As part of her studies to become an English teacher, she was required to come to the United States and participate in something where she would be immersed in the English language for a period of weeks. With her love of horses, the Ranch was a great fit.

Zack, who had been a friend of Brandon's since high school, had become like a son to Bill and I. Although this was his first summer working for us, he worked each of the following summer seasons. Zack worked as a wrangler, built fence and helped with the painting and general repairs around the Ranch. Zack has an outgoing personality that fit well with entertaining the guests.

As the season progressed, the staff seemed to enjoy their jobs and really enjoyed each other. After spending long days attending to guests, they still enjoyed spending time together in the evening. We often watched as they rode back into the Ranch together after a *night ride* or heard stories of the *parties in the A-frame*. The guys all bunked in the A-frame while the girls slept in the Wrangler's Quarters. The A-frame was a cabin that was built to look like the letter A, with one central peak. It had two floors and was big enough to house three or four wranglers. The Wrangler's Quarters was located near the horse pasture and attached to the tack room. Two wranglers slept in the Wrangler's Quarters comfortably.

Practical jokes were rampant between the two cabins throughout the season. Jeff was an easy target as he slept in a fold-up bed that hooked to the side of the

A-frame making it easy to hook him up while he was still sleeping. The guys scared the girls on several occasions by creating bear noises outside their cabin late at night. The girls teased Brandon unmercifully after his horse ran away while he was showing off and even went as far as to hang a wooden sign at the site where this happened. The sign read: Run-away Point.

As the summer progressed, Brandon and Jess seemed to be butting heads. Brandon was finding it difficult to be her boss and she was finding him just – difficult. Poor Tanja became the go-between and tried to keep the peace. It finally got so bad that Bill and I had to sit down and talk with both of them.

Several weeks after our talk, Bill and I were noticing more and more often that Brandon and Jess were holding hands. Although they tried to hide their affection toward each other while around us, it was quite apparent that what they had been fighting all summer was unfolding. They had fallen in love.

As the summer season drew to a close, it was time for Jess to return home to Virginia. Brandon and Jess spent a few days in Yellowstone National Park after which he drove her to the airport in Billings, Montana.

Brandon was miserable after Jess left. He went through the motions of his everyday chores, but it was obvious that something was missing. And, the tearful telephone messages left by Jess were evidence of the same feelings on her part.

Brandon came to me one morning and quietly broke the news. He was leaving the Ranch to join Jess in Virginia. The look on his face indicated that he thought

I would be upset with him for leaving the Ranch, but how could I be upset? He was young, he had fallen in love, and he had his whole life in front of him. It was a happy, but sad, day as he loaded his truck and headed off to Virginia a few weeks later. Bill and I had lost our right hand man, but we were also excited for Brandon and only wished the very best for him.

Third Summer Season 2001

Our third summer season began with our son Shane returning and taking over the head wrangler position. Shane handled the position well and filled the void that was left by Brandon's departure. Shane especially enjoyed working with a couple of the more difficult horses.

Shane was joined by our nephew, Scott, from Ohio. Scott is a tall, blonde, lanky guy whose strength was entertaining the guests. He was especially a hit with the young kids. Shane and Scott also spent every spare moment that summer cutting wood (providing our entire winter supply of wood before leaving at the end of the summer).

Brianna, Erica, Emily, and Tanja also joined our staff the third summer season. Brianna was from Colorado and we agreed to let her start her employment in May. May was always the time of year when we thoroughly cleaned the lodge and the cabins. Brianna joined right in helping me clean in preparation for the upcoming season. Shortly after Brianna started working for us she started dating one of the local guys from Greybull. Unfortunately as soon as the season started, she decided to take a job in Greybull where she would be closer to her boyfriend and where she would have the same day off as her boyfriend. And so the staffing problem began.

Erica was also from Colorado and had previously worked at several guest ranches. She had grown up around horses and worked out well as a wrangler. Erica was a tall, slender, blonde girl and soon became the attraction of a wrangler from another guest ranch located in Shell. Stewart was a tall, thin cowboy who reminded me of Jimmy Stewart. He sang and played a guitar and I hired him to replace Brandon, who previously provided music around the campfire on Friday nights. After a few weeks of singing for us, one day Stewart came galloping into the Ranch on his tall white horse. He asked if Erica was there. Unfortunately, she was out on a trail ride with guests. Stewart returned later that day and persuaded Erica to join him in the valley for dinner. Stewart and Erica continued dating throughout the summer.

Emily was from Ohio and assisted me in cleaning the cabins and helping in the kitchen that summer. She also coordinated the crafts for the children. Emily was easy going and enjoyed the activities at the Ranch. She often rode horses with the wranglers in the evenings and was comfortable leading the line-dancing night. She and Erica were known for their line dance, Cotton Eyed Joe, which took a lot of endurance. Emily was a few years older than the rest of the staff and they looked up to her.

Emily drove her Volkswagen Bug to the Ranch from Ohio. One day, she decided to drive to town and asked for directions to Greybull. Later in the day when she returned to the Ranch, she told us her story of her travels to Greybull. Instead of turning right out of the lane, she turned left which led her over the mountain road. The road is narrow with many deep ruts which could literally swallow up her little VW Bug. She told how she was in tears at one point until she decided to turn around and head back toward the Ranch.

Tanja, a wrangler from our previous season, joined us again a few weeks into the third season and she filled the void that was created by Brianna's departure. Tanja had become like a daughter to us. She was well-liked by the guests and was extremely comfortable with the horses. As the summer season progressed, it became evident that Scott and Tanja enjoyed each other's company. Unfortunately, this created hard feelings and one of our staff decided to leave. This left me without kitchen help and someone to clean the cabins. Thus the staffing problems continued.

Our daughter, Missy, joined us a few weeks later and took over the position of kitchen help and cabin clean up. Missy was especially great with the children and took over the children's activities, as well. She fit right in with the other staff and really rescued the staffing predicament for me as we had a large group scheduled for the week she arrived.

Fourth Summer Season 2002

We started our fourth summer season with all new staff. Billy and Nikki were from Vermont and were engaged to be married. Their wedding date was set for the fall after their first summer season working at the Ranch. Nikki was a good rider and had shown horses for several years back in Vermont. I have to say that Nikki was one of the easiest people to have work for us. She is a very mature person and was willing to do anything that was asked of her. She never complained (at least to me). Nikki is short with long, beautiful blonde hair. She was very comfortable in the saddle.

Billy is a tall, handsome guy with sandy brown hair. He was very ornery and eager to learn everything he could learn about the horses. Billy was especially comfortable around the guests and could talk to anyone. He and Nikki worked very hard and were a great asset to the Ranch.

Katie had stayed at the Ranch the previous summer as a guest with her parents. While a guest, she hung out with the wranglers and really enjoyed the Ranch life. As soon as she returned to Wisconsin, she applied for a position as a wrangler. We were pleased to hire Katie as, like Nikki, she was a real pleasure to work with and pitched in with every aspect of work needed. Although she wasn't hired as the Children's Wrangler, we quickly could see that she was great with the kids and had very creative ideas with the crafts. Katie was the girl next door with her strawberry blond, curly hair and freckles. She definitely had a fresh, fun loving approach to life and really cared about everyone's feelings. Katie also loved taking pictures and probably documented anything and everything that took place that summer.

Melissa was studying nursing at Clemson University in South Carolina and was hired as our Children's Wrangler. Melissa was of medium height with brown, straight hair and big, brown eyes. Melissa was a city girl and although she never complained about the duties as wrangler, it was obvious that she had seldom seen a pitch fork or used a rake. Melissa made up for her shortcomings with her personality and soon became comfortable around the horses. She was also comfortable talking to the guests and really enjoyed her summer at the Ranch.

Before the rest of the staff arrived, Bill and I traveled to Virginia to attend Brandon and Jess's wedding. On June 1, 2002, Brandon and Jess were married in a ceremony that took place high on a hilltop overlooking lush, rolling Virginia farmland. The bridesmaids rode into the ceremony in a horse drawn carriage. Jess, looking beautiful wearing her floor-length, white wedding dress, rode into the ceremony on a tall black horse while Brandon, wearing his Stetson hat, sang a song that he had written especially for her. Brandon and the groomsmen wore frock coats and cowboy boots. The western theme was carried throughout the reception.

Danny was a fifteen-year-old girl from Tennessee and was hired to assist me in the kitchen and with cleaning the cabins. Danny had jet black hair and dark eyes to match. She was a typical fifteen-year-old with lots of energy and kept me on my toes. She worked hard during her two month stint at the Ranch. Nikki took Danny under her wing and tried to keep her out of trouble, especially around the Moose. Danny tempted fate a few times while photographing the Moose and narrowly escaped through the fence with the Moose chasing her on one occasion. Danny was always eager to please and even took on the challenge of preparing dinner one evening for the guests and staff. Although there were a few tense moments, she pulled it off in her own special way. Danny was very confident for her age, sometimes creating her own problems. She dared Zack to race up the mountain, which ended with Danny hurting her knee a few days before she was to leave to go home.

Erica and Stewart were also married the previous fall and Erica came back for the summer to help out in the kitchen. Ethan, who had worked for another guest ranch in Shell, worked as a wrangler when we had large groups. Even though the core staff was all new faces, they worked together well and enjoyed both their work and their downtime together.

Tanja, Zack, Shane, and Missy also worked for us a few weeks here and there during the summer.

Soon after Melissa returned home at the end of the season, we received a letter from her mother. It seemed that Melissa was thinking of not returning to college, but had ideas of working on a ranch fulltime. Bill and I quickly emailed her and encouraged her to finish her college degree. Melissa finished college with a degree in Nursing and continued working on ranches during her college breaks. Eventually, Melissa moved to Colorado where she works as a nurse during the winter months, but returns to work on a ranch near Estes Park, Colorado, during the summer season.

Fifth Summer Season 2003

As our summer bookings increased, so did our need for staffing. We welcomed back Billy, Nikki, Katie, Missy, Tanja, and Zack for our fifth summer season and were excited to begin a new season with such fun loving, hardworking staff members who had become like family to Bill and me. In addition, our staffing developed a new twist when four (two couples) of our previous guests had inquired about coming to work for us during the 2003 season.

John and Anne were from Wisconsin. My first conversation with John was memorable because as I talked to him about our activities at the Ranch, he shared with me his love of the West and specifically his fascination with the *Lone Ranger*. He even admitted that among his collection of *Lone Ranger* memorabilia, was a replica of the complete outfit worn by the Lone Ranger himself.

Upon their arrival at the Ranch, as guests, John was excited to ride the horses and to share his knowledge and love of the old west characters with Bill. Anne was less enthusiastic about visiting the Ranch that summer. You might say that Anne was just along for the ride. Soon though, Anne opened up and shared with me her story of exploring the possibility of buying a bed and breakfast in their hometown of Beloit, Wisconsin. We talked about the pros and cons of owning your own business and especially the trials and tribulations of sharing your home with guests. We talked about how our faith had brought us to our decisions in going forward with our dreams.

As their Ranch vacation continued, Anne really settled in and thoroughly enjoyed the experience. She enjoyed the other guests, the beauty of the mountains surrounding the Ranch and as she began to bond with her horse, she felt more comfortable with the trail rides.

Shortly after returning home, John and Anne made reservations for a return trip to the Ranch the following summer. They both took riding lessons and even purchased their own horses. Bill and I were pleased to welcome John and Anne back to the Ranch the next summer and were intrigued when they quickly asked us to set aside some time to talk with them privately during their visit.

When we were able to meet with them, they expressed their desire to work for us the following summer. John was a school teacher and coach and Anne had just retired from a career as a nurse. Their plans were to work for a month for room and board in exchange for the experience of enjoying the Ranch. Anne offered to help in the kitchen while John's desire was working with the horses and assisting the wranglers. Bill and I were quite surprised. It had been difficult to find kitchen help and I was especially excited about the possibility of additional help in this area. We promised John and Anne that we would consider their proposal and talk with them further about the details that needed to be worked out.

Much to our surprise, Katie's parents, Mike and Joanie emailed us the same week to pose the same proposal of working for us the following summer. Mike is a fireman in his hometown of Pewaukee, Wisconsin, and Joanie is a nurse. They had visited the Ranch as guests the previous two summers. Mike looked like a cowboy with his tall, rugged build and his easy-going nature made him an easy fit at the Ranch. Joanie is a petite, fun loving person who, much like her daughter cared about everyone's feelings. And, the best part was that they both wanted to work in the kitchen. Hallelujah! For the first time since the beginning of the Ranch, I could actually walk away from the kitchen and feel comfortable that the guests would be well taken care of.

So the decision was made. John and Anne would work the first part of the summer season and Mike and Joanie would work the second part of the summer season. They both brought their own campers to live in making the logistical issues much simpler. It truly was like sharing our Ranch with family.

Like family, there were a few bumps along the way. A few times the staff had to be reminded that the Ranch was our place of business and that Bill and I made the decisions. And, allowing the wranglers to raid the cookie jar was something that I both enjoyed and allowed even though it was not always tolerated by the new kitchen help. The issues were quickly worked out and life went on.

Bill and I would celebrate our thirtieth wedding anniversary this year and I had secretly planned a celebration. Well before the staff arrived at the Ranch, I had contacted the female staff to invite them to share in this celebration and solicited their help with a few aspects of the preparations.

The celebration was planned during a week that our sons, Shane and Brandon, along with Brandon's wife Jess were visiting the Ranch. Missy, our granddaughter Emma, and Zack were already there as staff members. In addition, several of our kid's friends were visiting from Ohio and Kansas. All of our family and extended family were in attendance. It was perfect!

It was a beautiful day on the mountain, with bright blue skies and seventy degree temperatures as Bill and I stood before our family and repeated our wedding vows. Tony, a long-time family friend and pastor of a church in nearby Sheridan, Wyoming, presided over the ceremony. We stood in front of the split rail fence decorated by Missy and Nikki with the backdrop of the mountains beyond us. Each cabin had received a handmade invitation to the ceremony, made and delivered by Katie and Tanja. Anne had prepared delicious food for the occasion and Katie had painstakingly prepared a beautiful wedding cake. The dining room was decorated with flower arrangements purchased in the nearby town of Greybull. Jeff acted as the photographer and when the DJ didn't show up, Zack saved the day by acting as DJ. Following dinner and the cutting of the cake, we danced under the stars until late into the night.

Looking back, that day and the love that was shared between my family and the staff was one of my most memorable of all of our days at the Ranch. What a blessing that day remains in my heart.

Also, while our family and extended family were visiting the Ranch, the nearby town of Basin was holding its annual county fair. Katie and Nikki had talked Missy and Tanja into entering the pig wrestling contest with them. We all piled into vehicles and made the trek to Basin to cheer them on.

Watching the girls try to wrestle the mud covered pigs into the assigned pen was too comical for words. Slipping and sliding in the muddy, wet arena, while attempting to catch the squirmy little pigs proved too much for the girls. They were covered from head to toe with the mud and gunk. Although they didn't win, we all thoroughly enjoyed watching the contest. And, the girls made some fun memories in the process.

The most delightful part of this summer season was our granddaughter, Emma. Missy and Emma came to stay with us in May and remained at the Ranch until after hunting season. Emma was such a joy to have around. Not only did Bill and I get to spend every day with her, but the guests enjoyed her as well. She was only five months old when they came in May and we were overjoyed to experience some of her firsts. Having Emma and Missy at the Ranch helped to ease my homesick feelings.

Sixth Summer Season 2004

Billy, Nikki, and Katie returned to work at the Ranch as wranglers for their third consecutive year. Richard was hired to work with me in the kitchen. Ant, Rebecca, Liz, and Suzi also joined the staff along with Zack who worked part of the summer. Our weeks during the summer season had filled quickly and we were accommodating larger groups of guests. It was reassuring to have seasoned wranglers along with the extra help that could be used wherever the need arose.

Richard is the brother of a good friend of our son Brandon and had visited the Ranch during our anniversary celebration. Richard is large in stature, standing at six-foot-four, but a teddy bear at heart. Richard teaches school and really loves to cook. Armed with his favorite barbeque sauce, he dug right in and kicked the kitchen up a notch. I could depend on him not only to cook a great meal, but also to assist me in keeping the kitchen well stocked. Richard was from Wichita, Kansas. During his stay at the Ranch, he typed all of my favorite Ranch recipes into the computer.

Liz and Suzi were from the state of Michigan and were high school friends. They had both just graduated from high school and were planning to attend college in the fall. Liz's Uncle Bob lived in Cody, Wyoming. He was the real estate agent that represented the seller of the Ranch when we purchased it and we had become good friends. Bob had talked to us about Liz and Suzi working for us for part of the summer and had even provided a camper for them to live in during their stay at the Ranch. So, Liz and Suzi worked part of the summer season and Ant and Rebecca filled in the remainder of the summer season. Liz and Suzie were two of the nicest, well-mannered, fun loving young girls that I had ever met. They were both comfortable on a horse and they also were able to divide their time between helping in the kitchen, cleaning the cabins, and riding as wranglers.

Bill graduated from The Ohio State University and we both are Ohio State Buckeye fans. Since Liz and Suzi both are from Michigan and University of Michigan fans, we joked often about our favorite teams. At the end of the season Bill received a University of Michigan ball cap as a momento of their visit.

Ant and Rebecca had been previous guests. They are from England and had vacationed with us two previous years. Ant is a teacher and was able to spend a month at the Ranch. When it was time for Liz and Suzi to return home, Ant and Rebecca took over in their place, dividing their time between helping in the kitchen, cleaning the cabins, and riding as wranglers. I was thrilled to have the extra help and they were excited to spend time on the Ranch.

Erik, Katie's boyfriend, drove Katie out to the Ranch and a few of his friends came along to keep him company on the long ride back to Wisconsin. They arrived the day that the leased horses were delivered. Although Erik and his friends were not familiar with horses, Erik assisted while Bill and the wranglers ran the horses up the road to the Ranch. One of Erik's friends had decided to return to the Ranch by walking the steep mile up the narrow road. Bill commented later that as the thirty horses ran past this guy on a narrow stretch of the road, the look on his face was priceless. He was rather startled as he witnessed the sight of thirty horses running past him at full speed as he stood just a few feet away clinging to a tree.

Wild Bill

The dream that started with Brandon quickly became Bill's dream. Bill relied on his background as an accountant and C.P.A. to gather the information and research the viability of ranch ownership. Bill's education and prior business experience greatly enhanced our ability to purchase the Ranch. But once the decision was made to pursue the Ranch, Bill took on the persona of Wild Bill.

History has always been important to Bill. From researching his ancestry to learning more about the rich history of the Ranch, Bill's love for both of those things grew with the purchase of Ranger Creek Guest Ranch. He loved to research the history of the Ranch and pass it on to his family and the guests. The guests enjoyed visits with Wild Bill to historic places such as Little Big Horn, The Medicine Wheel, Dinosaur Digs, and Cody, Wyoming (the home of Buffalo Bill). Bill continued learning about the area and we visited many of the historic sites which Bill then passed on to the guests.

Often on our drives back to Ohio to visit our family, Bill and I brainstormed about ideas for improvements to the Ranch and the summer activities. We attempted to incorporate much of the history of the area in the Ranch activities. The area had so much to offer and we both enjoyed sharing it with the guests.

While running the Ranch, Bill was not afraid to ask for help. If he was unsure about an issue with the horses, he solicited help from those who grew up with horses and worked with them on a daily basis. Tom Sharpe, the realtor who found the Ranch for us, was one of Bill's sources. Tom had grown up in the West and is a true cowboy in every sense of the word. When Tom wasn't showing a property, he was working cattle or training horses. He visited the Ranch often and not only helped to train a few of our horses, but offered guidance to Bill whenever he needed it. Tom has become a valued friend over the years and we both feel blessed to know him.

During the summer season the guests thoroughly enjoyed Wild Bill's impression of Buffalo Bill Cody. Wild Bill would ride across the pasture and up to the campfire on his horse Duke. Dressed in a handmade fringed leather coat, vest, and woolen pants, Wild Bill engaged the guests with his impression of the days and times of Buffalo Bill. With the backdrop of the Ranch, the adults and especially the children were captivated by Wild Bill's impression that took them back in history to a time seen only in the movies.

I always said that Bill should have been an actor because he was comfortable being in the spotlight. Marketing himself through our Ranch brochures, newsletter, website, and emails, the kids especially could not wait to meet Wild Bill upon their arrival to the Ranch. He became like a super hero in their minds through the setting of the Ranch and the history that he shared with them. Wild Bill and Brandon even sang around the campfire the first couple of years with their rendition of *Poncho and Lefty*.

Wild Bill developed a professional connection with Ranch America, a travel group out of the United Kingdom, which resulted in numerous bookings over the years. The owner of Ranch America came to visit the Ranch and included a picture of Wild Bill dressed in his buckskin coat and Stetson hat in his marketing brochure.

Wild Bill loved to ride horses and enjoyed sharing his love of riding and his love of nature with the guests. Whether it was a short trail ride with a drop-in guest or an all-day ride to Shell Reservoir, Wild Bill ensured that the guests were at ease and enjoyed themselves by pointing out the wildlife or points of interest along the way. For the more advanced riders, Wild Bill thoroughly enjoyed kicking it up and giving the guests the full adventure by galloping through the sage brush and along the mountain trails. He especially loved racing the staff and the guests with his horse Duke, who was difficult to beat.

The staff enjoyed working with Wild Bill and especially loved playing practical jokes on him. He oftentimes would come down to the paddock in the morning after breakfast to find his saddle on his horse backwards, his saddle bags full of rocks, or one stirrup higher than the other. Duke was a good sport when they braided his mane and tied it up with ribbons. Upon coming off his horse one day because his cinch was loosely fastened, the wranglers feared they had gone too far, but Wild Bill calmly climbed back on his horse and stated, "Paybacks are hell!"

The staff and I often teased Wild Bill about his unending desire to talk to people. If Wild Bill wasn't riding a horse, you could most often find him sitting on the front porch of the lodge talking to the guests. During our weekly trips to Cody with our guests, if given the opportunity, Wild Bill would strike up a conversation with the person standing next to him. Whether he was shopping in a store, sitting on the porch of the Irma Hotel or waiting to cross the street, he never passed up an opportunity to talk to anyone and market the Ranch whenever the opportunity arose.

Another way Wild Bill marketed the Ranch during the winter season was by offering lunch to the snowmobilers that were playing on our side of the mountain. While they were there for lunch Wild Bill talked to them and showed them around the Ranch. On one particular day, I was making homemade beef and noodles, which took most of the day to prepare. Brandon and Wichita, our winter staff, were there and also Zack was visiting with a couple of friends. We were all looking forward to the beef and noodles for dinner. Later in the afternoon, well after lunch time, a large group of snowmobilers stopped by. While Bill was chatting with them, he asked them if they were interested in lunch. Smelling the aroma of the beef and noodles cooking in the kitchen the group inquired about what I was cooking. Wild Bill proceeded to sell them the entire pot of beef and noodles. Needless to say, he got into a little bit of trouble over that one.

Wild Bill often commented that although he enjoyed the spotlight, his favorite part of the day was his early morning rides to gather the horses on the mountain. The beauty and the quietness of the mountain provided a perfect way to start the day.

During the winter months at the Ranch Wild Bill wrote a book about his ancestry entitled *History of the Ancestors, Families and Descendants of Paris Patrick Comisford.* The book was published in 2007 by Heritage Books.

Riding Programs and Activities

Ranger Creek Guest Ranch and the scenic area that surrounded the Ranch provided a perfect vacation spot for individuals, couples, and families to get a way from the normal hustle and bustle of life and to relax and enjoy nature at its best. While setting up our activities, we firmly believed that our programs needed to build off of the natural surroundings and enhance the experience of our guests by providing activities and programs that engulfed the wholesome nature already present at the Ranch. Our programs grew and changed overtime as our business grew and our own knowledge of the area expanded. But, in general our program followed these general guidelines.

Sunday

3:00	Welcome & Registration
4:00	Orientation Ride
6:00	Dinner in the Lodge
7:00	Ice Cream Social on the Front Porch

Monday

8:30	Breakfast in the Lodge
9:30	Ride to Eagles Nest
12:00	Lunch in the Lodge
1:30	Ride to Shell Creek Water Crossing

3:30   Cowboy Crafts
6:00   Dinner in the Lodge
7:00   Wild Flowers of the Big Horn Mountains

Tuesday

8:00   Breakfast Ride
12:00   Lunch in the Lodge
2:00   Ride to Cow Pond
3:30   Cowboy Crafts
6:00   Dinner in the Lodge
7:00   Line Dancing in the Lodge

Wednesday

8:30   Breakfast in the Lodge
10:30   Ride to Shell Creek
12:00   Lunch along Shell Creek
2:00   Ride back to Ranch
3:30   Cowboy Crafts
6:00   Dinner in the Lodge
7:00   Visit by Buffalo Bill Cody (as presented by
        Wild Bill) Woodcarving Presentation (as
        presented by Ernie & Iona)
8:00   Overnights were available to the guests at a
        campsite near the Ranch

Thursday

8:30   Breakfast in the Lodge
9:30   Ridge Ride
12:00   Lunch in the Lodge
1:30   Trip to Cody, Wyoming, for shopping and
        sightseeing
5:30   Pizza in Cody
7:00   Cody Nite Rodeo

Friday

8:30   Breakfast in the Lodge
9:30   Ride to Crooked Creek Canyon
12:00   Lunch in the Lodge
2:30   Ranch Rodeo (barrel racing and cowboy games)
6:00   Dinner around the campfire
7:00   Cowboy Singing (as provided by Wild Bill, Brandon, Peanut, & Stewart)

Saturday

8:30   Breakfast in the Lodge Farewells and tearful goodbyes.

Cowboy Crafts: Crafts designed around a cowboy theme for little cowboys and cowgirls ages ten and under, although many older cowboys and cowgirls enjoyed them as well. Crafts included candle holders, flimsy stained glass, bandanas, horseshoe decorating, dream catchers, beaded necklaces, and bracelets.

Wild Flower Presentation: Dave and Jean Anderson, National Forest Interpreters from Shell Falls, shared their beautiful voices and their love of wildflowers with our guests. Through song, wildflower slide show, and a walk around the Ranch, Dave and Jean provided a glimpse of the beauty of nature surrounding Ranger Creek Guest Ranch.

Line Dancing: Line dancing night was an activity that was planned out and introduced our very first summer by wranglers Brandon, Kayleen, and Peanut. Dances were added and subtracted depending on the comfort level of the guests. Our very own "Ranger Creek Line Dance" was introduced our second summer by wranglers Brandon, Zack, Shane, Jeff, Jess, and Tanja. Favorite line dances included: Boot Scootin' Boogie, Electric Slide, Ranger Creek Line Dance, and Sway.

Shopping & Visit to Buffalo Bill Cody Historical Center in Cody, Wyoming: Shopping in the historic western town of Cody, Wyoming, or spending a few hours in the Buffalo Bill Cody Historical Center. The center is a shrine to Buffalo Bill Cody and to the early pioneers of the American West.

Cody Nite Rodeo: The Cody Nite Rodeo offers two hours of rodeo events including Saddle Bronc Riding, Bareback Riding, Steer Wrestling, Team Roping, Barrel Racing and Bull Riding.

Woodcarving Presentation: Ernie and Iona Smith produced beautiful carvings of bear, eagle, and other wildlife for the guests' enjoyment. Ernie was well known for his chainsaw carvings and had won several national awards. The guests were able to purchase the carvings created for them as they watched.

Overnights: Sleeping under the beautiful Wyoming stars was one of the activities available to guests staying at our Ranch. Guests rode their horses through the forest of lodge pole pines and stopped along the trail where they camped for the night. Dinner was provided by the Ranch staff and served at the campsite. Following dinner and an evening around the campfire, the guests slept either in tents or under the starlit sky.

Riding Program

Orientation Ride: The orientation ride was the first ride the guests experienced. This ride was a short ride on rather flat trails along the logging roads with few obstacles. This ride provided an opportunity for the rider to feel comfortable in the saddle and get to know their horse. Just as important, it gave the wranglers a chance to make sure they had the guest matched with the right horse and the saddle was properly adjusted. This ride wound through tall lodge pole pines and often provided opportunity to observe wildlife such as moose, elk, and deer.

Eagles Nest: The ride to Eagles Nest tested the riders' skill as they climbed farther up the mountain on their horse, navigating rocks and sagebrush along the way. Eagles Nest is an outcropping of rocks that lay at an altitude of approximately 9000 feet and overlooks the Ranch. The view from Eagles Nest was spectacular and one could see for miles down Shell Canyon. This outcropping of rocks had earned the name Eagles Nest decades before our ownership of the Ranch. Early in the spring, baby eagles could be seen learning how to fly as their mommas gently scooted them out of the nest for the first time.

Shell Creek Water Crossing: The trail to Shell Creek began with climbing the hill behind the paddock area. Once up and over the top of the hill, the steep descent down the backside of the hill was slow and steady but worth the wait as the trail crossed a meadow of wildflowers. During the months of June and July, lupine and balsam root provided a picturesque scene of yellow and purple. Topping off the splendor of the wildflowers was the crystal clear water of Shell Creek as the winter run off rushed through the canyon. After crossing a narrow bridge over Shell Creek the trail followed alongside the creek down past the summer cabins.

Breakfast Ride: The breakfast ride circled behind the Ranch climbing through the pine trees just below the base of the massive granite peaks that lay above and behind the Ranch. It was a normal occurrence to meet up with moose during this early morning ride. The trail ride ended at the breakfast site located just inside the entrance to the Ranch where guests were eager for a hearty breakfast cooked in an oversized iron skillet over an open fire.

Cow Pond: The trail to the cow pond weaved through lush green pasture continually climbing to altitudes of 9,100 feet. The cow pond was a man made pond dug for the purpose of watering cattle that openly graze on the mountain grasses in the summer. The views from the cow pond provide an exquisite picture of the Cloud Peak Wilderness Area in the distance. Through most of the summer months the peaks will be covered in snow.

Shell Creek Lunch Site: The trail weaved down the mountain and through the pine forest along the lower logging road ending at a peaceful spot along Shell Creek. Guests enjoyed hot soup cooked over an open fire and served in tin cups. A table decorated with gingham tablecloths and fresh flowers was laden with corn bread muffins, warm chocolate chip cookies, and cool lemonade. Guests enjoyed the sound of the babbling mountain stream and the routine glimpse of moose grazing along the creek as they ate their lunch.

Ridge Ride: Climbing the hill behind the paddock area, the trail proceeded farther up the mountain and behind the massive granite peaks that rose above and behind the Ranch. The trail was steep as it switched back and forth across the heavily wooded area. It was so steep that the horses routinely tucked their behinds and slid as they climbed back down the trail. Where the forest ended, the trail took a sharp turn to the left and followed the ridge of the mountain around to an opening in another clump of trees. The ridge was narrow and approximately forty feet long with sharp drop offs to 120 foot depths below. Picturesque views extending for up to eight miles down Shell Canyon lay below the Ridge. Once through the trees, the trail opened up into a broad high mountain meadow.

The guests had to prove that they could handle their horse before the wranglers would allow them to make this ride. Although many choose not to participate in this ride, for those who did experience the ridge ride, it was their badge of courage. Once experiencing the ridge ride climbing up the mountain, many riders elected not to experience it climbing back down the mountain. If the rider was comfortable crossing the ridge, the views down Shell Canyon were incredible. The youngest rider that experienced the ridge ride was five years old and the oldest was eighty-five.

Crooked Creek Canyon: The wide meadow that wraps around through Crooked Creek Canyon provides the perfect place to let the guests kick it up and run with the horses. This picturesque canyon was used in early days as the Mail Trail along the old stagecoach road. Riders carried mail on horseback through the canyon from Sheridan to Cody.

All Day Rides to Shell Reservoir: For the more experienced riders, Wild Bill or one of the wranglers would take them on an all-day ride to Shell Reservoir. This ride began with the ride down to Shell Creek Water Crossing. The riders then followed Shell Creek back up through the canyon as it curled its way up the mountain to Shell Reservoir. The reservoir sat at an elevation of 9,000 feet. The run off from the winter snows created the crystal clear water of this reservoir. Depending on the time of year, the water could easily cover the dam. Or, as the season progressed, could be shallow in spots. From a certain spot on the road leading into the reservoir you could see three lakes: the reservoir; Lake Adelaide, and Shell Lake. It provided an exquisite photo opportunity.

The Big Horn Mountains offered a wide variety of sporting and sightseeing options. Trout fishing in the numerous lakes and streams located in the Big Horn Mountains was one of the favorite activities of the men and white water rafting trips were enjoyed by many of the groups that visit the Ranch. Other sightseeing trips included:

The Medicine Wheel: Situated atop Medicine Mountain at an elevation of 9,642 feet in Wyoming's

Big Horn Mountains, the Medicine Wheel attracts thousands of visitors each year. The wheel itself measures nearly eighty feet in diameter and consists of twenty-eight alignments of limestone boulders radiating from a central cairn associated with six smaller stone enclosures found around the wheel's perimeter. While the exact purpose of the wheel, its age, and the identity of its makers are unknown, researchers believe the wheel was constructed over a period of centuries from about 1,500 to about 500 years ago.

The land surrounding the wheel has been used by prehistoric American Indian groups for at least 7,000 years. In contemporary times, the region's Arapaho, Bannock, Blackfeet, Cheyenne, Crow, Kootenai-Salish, Lakota Sioux, Plains Cree, Shoshone, and other tribal people generally venerate to the site and some use it to fast, pray, and experience vision quests.

Little Big Horn: Commonly known as Custer's Last Stand. The location of the battle between combined forces of Lakota, Northern Cheyenne, and Arapaho tribes against the 7th Calvary Regiment of the U.S. Army on June 25 and 26, 1876, along the Little Big Horn River.

Dinosaur Digs, Shell, Wyoming: The Red Gulch Dinosaur Tracksite near Shell, Wyoming, is the largest dinosaur tracksite in Wyoming, and one of two Middle Jurassic age tracksites known in the world. The tracksite area contains literally thousands of rare Middle Jurassic age dinosaur tracks embedded in oolitic limestone. Located on public land near Shell, Wyoming, this site covers forty acres set-aside by the USDI-Bureau of Land Management.

Pryor Mountain Wild Horse Range: The Bureau of Land Management's Pryor Mountain Wild Horse Range is located on the south slope of East Pryor Mountain overlooking the Bighorn Basin of Wyoming. In addition to searching for the Pryor Mustangs, the rugged and mysterious Pryor Mountain country beckons the adventuresome to explore over the next ridge- into the next draw- for what might be discovered in this out-of-the-way land that few have visited.

Approximately 120 wild horses range from the Pryors' high meadows down through rugged juniper-covered foothills to colorful desert-like badlands that border the green fields of Crooked Creek Valley. The many ridges and ravines give the mustangs room to roam and finding them is not guaranteed.

The Singing Rangers
of the Big Horn
Mountains

Dave and Jean were National Forest Rangers in the Big
Horn Mountains for thirteen years. Upon retiring from
their teaching careers in Nebraska, they made a decision to sell their home and most of their possessions
and purchased a fifth wheel camper. The purchase of
the fifth wheel enabled them to travel to the West during the summer months and to the South during the
winter months.

In 1990, they began their career as National Forest
Rangers and were stationed at Shell Falls. They ran the
gift shop as well as greeted travelers that stopped by to
observe the splendor of the beautiful water falls known
as Shell Falls. The center at Shell Falls receives an esti-
mated 350,000 visitors a year.

Dave and Jean had been given the gift of beautiful
voices and they also had a great love of wild flowers. They
used both of these gifts to entertain and teach the curious travelers who stopped at Shell Falls. Tour buses and
single vehicles alike were sure to make Shell Falls one
of their stops along their journey through the Big Horn
Mountains. Dave and Jean had gained the reputation of
The Singing Rangers of the Big Horn Mountains.

Shell Falls became a frequent stop with our guests where we were treated to beautiful music. Many of the songs were written by Dave. Over dinner one evening, Dave shared with Bill and me that over the years he had accumulated hundreds of slides of wildflowers and shared many comical stories of his passion for photographing wildflowers. Jean told of how he embarrassed their two young daughters by holding up a long line of traffic while he stopped to photograph a certain wildflower along the road in Yellowstone National Park.

Their enthusiasm and joyful nature was contagious and during one of their visits to the Ranch, Bill asked Dave and Jean if they would be interested in coming up to the Ranch once a week to share their wildflower slides and their voices with our guests. To our delight, Dave and Jean quickly agreed.

The Singing Rangers of the Big Horn Mountains became a regular activity on Monday evening. After joining us and our guests for dinner, Dave and Jean presented their slide show of picturesque wildflowers coupled with songs of the beautiful nature of the Big Horn Mountains, sprinkled with Jean's telltale stories about Dave and his antics to obtain the perfect picture. Needless to say, they were an immediate hit with our guests. They were lovingly referred to as *the singing Rangers* or *that wildflower guy*.

Early one day, Dave stopped by the Ranch concerned that his projector was not working. He told me that they would need to cancel their presentation. Knowing how disappointed the guests would be, I suggested that instead of showing the slides, perhaps he could walk around the Ranch and point out the wildflowers to the guests. During the months of May, June, July, and even as late as August, the wildflowers were everywhere. Dave took a quick walk around the Ranch and enthusiastically agreed to substitute a walk through the wildflowers in place of the slide show. Our guests that evening were even more delighted by the wildflower walk and Dave and Jean adopted the walk as part of their regular presentation. By walking through the Ranch with Dave pointing out the wildflowers, the guests became even more aware of the flowers around them. To add more fun, Dave instituted a challenge to the guests, find a wildflower that he could *not* identify. Rarely was Dave unable to quickly identify the wildflower pointed out to him. Dave also taught the guests the importance of not picking the flowers (especially around Shell Falls where so many travelers passed through), but leaving them to promulgate to create beauty for years to come in the mountains.

As was often the case, I would hear many of the men guests tell their wives before the presentation that they would probably not be interested in the wildflower walk, but would attend for a few minutes in an attempt not to appear rude. Most of the time, Dave and Jean quickly hooked these men and they were searching along with the other guests for a wildflower to stump Dave. They became so interested that they began noticing and even searching out the wildflowers while on horseback.

One such guest, in an attempt to identify a wildflower, walked to the top of a steep hill in the pasture area not once, but twice to try to remember and explain the look of the wildflower. Dave finally told him to pick the flower and bring it to him, which he did, climbing the steep hill a third time to retrieve it. Dave quickly identified the flower, much to Ron's delight.

Dave and Jean truly loved their job, the Big Horn Mountains and wild flowers. Their love of nature easily spilled over to our staff and guests and we are all blessed to have known and shared this time with them.

Ranger Creek Ranch Rodeo

A rodeo for children with life threatening illnesses and their families

As you can imagine, Brandon's diagnosis of cancer changed our family's life. During Brandon's treatment and the complications that followed, the fear and uncertainty about our son's future could have easily taken over and destroyed our lives. But, the support we received from family, friends, our church, our community, and even people we had never met, allowed us to face the fear with confidence. God had placed all of these people in our lives for a reason and with their support we grew stronger as a family. We often talked about how we could pay back the kindness and support that was shown to us during this difficult time in our lives. Once the decision was made to purchase the Ranch, we immediately began to talk about how we could incorporate a program at the Ranch that would lend support to families dealing with a childhood illness.

Woody Hayes, the well-known football coach at The Ohio State University, introduced a phrase called, Paying It Forward. Bill quickly embraced this phrase and envisioned a program which we called Ranger Creek Ranch Rodeo. This yearly rodeo event became our way of paying forward to others in similar circumstance all the love, blessings, and support that was shown to us during our son's illness.

Our first Ranger Creek Ranch Rodeo was held in September following our first summer season at the Ranch. Bill worked with The Make-A-Wish Foundation in Casper, Wyoming, and a local pediatrician in Sheridan, Wyoming, to identify children with life threatening illnesses and their families. Volunteers from the neighboring communities of Sheridan, Shell, and Greybull flooded our Ranch with support. The Market Warehouse in Sheridan supplied all the groceries for the weekend so that I could prepare meals for the families and the volunteers. Another grocery store in Greybull supplied all the paper products. Cowboys from Greybull and Shell volunteered as wranglers and brought along their horses. Another guest ranch in Shell sent up several horses and a few of their wranglers. Tony, a friend of ours from Sheridan, provided a sound system and helped out throughout the day. Jim, a local rodeo clown from Basin, provided entertainment. Tom Sharpe, our friend and realtor from Colorado drove 700 miles to lend his support and brought along his horses, as well.

The families arrived on Friday evening. Following registration, where the children were given rodeo t-shirts, the families were given a quick tour of the Ranch and shown to their cabins. Refreshments were served in the lodge and the families were given a chance to get to know one another and the Ranger

Creek Guest Ranch staff. The first night the children had a slumber party in the lodge while their parents enjoyed some quiet time in their cabin.

Following breakfast in the lodge on Saturday morning, the children as well as the parents enjoyed a trail ride. Each child was matched with a wrangler for the day, who assisted them in feeling comfortable on their horse and accompanied them on the trail rides and with all the activities throughout the day.

Following lunch in the lodge, the much anticipated Ranger Creek Ranch Rodeo took place in the pasture just in front of the lodge. Barrel racing, cowboy games, steer roping, relay races, marshmallow eating contests, and entertainment by the rodeo clown were among the favorite activities. Parents and on-lookers from the community gathered in front of the lodge with their lawn chairs to enjoy the activities.

In the evening, everyone gathered around a campfire to enjoy hotdogs, marshmallows, and delicious side dishes created by the Ranger Creek Guest Ranch kitchen staff. Singing around the campfire as well as Tom, our favorite cowboy poet, reciting a few of his own poems helped create a memorable day for the children and their families.

Following breakfast in the lodge on Sunday morning, the tired and tearful children and their parents said their goodbyes and departed the Ranch with wonderful memories of a weekend that they would not soon forget.

It was heartwarming to experience the weekend and watch the bond that was created between the children and the volunteers that shared this experience with them year after year. I fondly recall as Loren, an older cowboy from Shell, tearfully shared with me how he truly enjoyed this weekend and looked forward to it each and every year.

In subsequent years, we began holding our Ranger Creek Ranch Rodeo on the first weekend of the summer season because we felt it was the perfect way to kick off our summer season.

Dr. John Stamato, an Oncologist in Sheridan, Wyoming wrote: "What a great time for all! Your "Ranch Rodeo," a get-a-way for children and their families who have fought, or are currently fighting the battle against cancer, was a huge success! It was an opportunity for families and children to get together, to share a common bond, and an opportunity for us all to open up our hearts. Thank you Bill and Sue for opening up your hearts, for graciously offering your splendid ranch for this purpose. I felt privileged to be part of it. Thank you!"

The first year we held the Ranch Rodeo, only one wish child was able to make the trip. Due to illness, car problems, and other schedules, the other families were unable to attend the rodeo. Our decision to move the Ranch Rodeo to June attributed to a steady increase in attendance. Each of the following years the attendance grew and during the last year we held the Ranch Rodeo, twenty-one children attended. Listed below are just a few of the stories of these brave children with whom we are privileged to have shared our lives and the Ranch.

Kassie, eleven, and Mike, her thirteen-year-old brother, drove from Casper, Wyoming, with their parents to participate in the 1st Annual Ranch Rodeo. After a year of fighting to survive cancer, Kassie was in remission after a diagnosis of T-cell, non-Hodgkin's Lymphoma. Kassie would like the chance to give other children hope and share her experience. She is also inspired to become a pediatric oncologist because she'd understand the patients, not just what's wrong with them.

Kalani and his family were from Houston, Texas. Kalani's aunt lived in Buffalo, Wyoming, and heard about our Ranch Rodeo through the hospital where she worked. After hearing about Kalani's battle with cancer, we invited Kalani and his family to participate in the Ranch Rodeo. Kalani was fourteen when he first attended the Ranch Rodeo and had been dealing with cancer since he was seven. Kalani attended the Ranch Rodeo the next few years and had such a great time that he asked if he could come to the Ranch for his senior trip. We enjoyed having Kalani spend a week at the Ranch later in the summer where he enjoyed riding horses. The wranglers took Kalani under their wing and made him feel like part of the family.

Theresa and her family lived in Worland, Wyoming, and she came to the Ranch Rodeo with her triplet sisters. Theresa was nine and had been free of cancer for a year before attending the 2nd Annual Ranch Rodeo. Bill and I looked forward to seeing Theresa, Victoria, and Katherine every year along with their parents and celebrating another healthy year for Theresa.

Brittney was ten when she first attended the Ranch Rodeo. Brittney had been dealing with cancer since she was one. Brain tumors now prevented Brittney from speaking, but she enjoyed being lead around the corral by Wrangler Zack and her father, Rick. Brittney especially enjoyed when Brandon sang to her around the campfire later that evening.

Codi was twelve when she attended the 2nd Annual Ranch Rodeo. Codi has a blood disorder which caused her to lose half her foot the previous year. Codi traveled to the Ranch from Dubois, Wyoming, with her sisters, Jodi and Tobi and her mom and dad. None of the sisters were thinking of the blood disorder that Saturday, they were learning to rope, ride, and barrel race.

Clayton from Casper, Wyoming, was six and had a stem cell transplant for AMI, leukemia the previous year. While attending the 4th Annual Ranch Rodeo, his father commented, "Clayton liked being able to ride a horse. He thought it was fun. He had been on a horse when he was about two, but didn't remember it."

In addition to the Ranch Rodeo, Bill and I also had the honor of making two children's wishes come true by hosting the child and their families for a week vacation at the Ranch organized by The Make-A-Wish Foundation.

Wyatt, his nine-year-old sister, Shayla, and his mom and dad visited the Ranch in July of 2003. Wyatt was five years old and had been dealing with surgeries and cancer treatments for nine months previous to coming to the Ranch. Wyatt and his family were from Tekamah, Nebraska. Brenda, his mother, stated, "Because of his hospital stays, Wyatt always wants to go home. But he never once asked to go home while we were there. This wasn't just Wyatt's dream; it was a dream for all of us. If I had any concerns, they knew what to do. You couldn't ask for better people to be with your children."

Moriah and her family of seven visited us in August of 2004 from South Carolina. Moriah was five and had been dealing with cancer treatment for well over a year prior to their visit. Moriah had big blue eyes and could easily flash her eyes at anyone and get exactly what she wanted. Moriah's little brother, Seth, came to the Ranch dressed in his cowboy outfit, complete with a cowboy hat and toy pistol. At the end of their visit, Seth could not be found. He was hiding in one of the cabins because he didn't want to leave the Ranch.

Wildlife

During our quest to purchase a guest ranch, I grew concerned with the possibility of purchasing a ranch that was in Grizzly country. The Big Horn Mountains are not in grizzly country, but they are heavily populated with black bear. As one forest ranger told me, black bears can be just as dangerous as grizzly bears.

Our first encounter with black bear took place one night just after dark. Bill's brother, Randy, was visiting the Ranch and he and Bill were walking back to the Lodge. They noticed that a number of horses were lined up at the cowboy gate seemingly watching something near the storage shed. We were storing the garbage in this shed until time permitted the building of a proper garbage bin. After drawing our attention to what was taking place and hearing banging noises coming from inside the building, Randy threw a rock at the building. Suddenly, a bear scrambled out the window of the shed and slid between the shed and a nearby stack of hay. The horses immediately took off running. The bear also decided the garbage wasn't worth the hassle and made its way down through the pasture.

The garbage bin quickly made its way to the top of the to-do list and a large metal garbage bin was built. As predicted by the forest rangers, about a week later we were awakened by a barking dog. Our dogs usually spent the night inside the lodge, but that particular night, Cali, our Alaskan Malamute was left outside.

When Bill went to see what Cali was barking about, he noticed some movement around the garbage bin. The bear was back. As we watched from the lodge, the bear pushed and pulled on the bin in an effort to gain access to its contents. After a few minutes of pushing and pulling, he backed away resting on his front paws with his hind end in the air as if to study the situation. Finally giving up on the garbage bin, he headed up the short incline to the lodge. On the side porch of the lodge was a grill and a refrigerator. At that time, the refrigerator contained forty pounds of hamburger among other things. The bear made his way to the porch and headed for the smells coming from the grill. Putting his paws all over the grill and then moving on to the refrigerator. As we watched from the window, we prayed that he would not figure out how to open the refrigerator. If he did, we would never get rid of him. The bear seemed to notice us watching him and looked through the window directly at us. Zack had snagged his video camera when he heard the commotion, but in all his excitement forgot to turn the camera on.

Finally, the bear made his way around the lodge and just when we thought he was leaving, he walked over to the Suburban and put his paws on the top of it as he looked through the windows. Bill banged on some pots and pans outside the front of the lodge causing him to mosey down the lane.

Later when talking with the forest rangers, they explained that the reason he looked inside the Suburban was because several campers (from the campgrounds just below the Ranch) had left food inside their cars with the windows slightly open. The bear had snapped the windows to gain access to the food inside. The bear was looking for food in our Suburban.

Another very late evening Bill had picked up guests at the airport. When they arrived back at the Ranch, Bill noticed the recycle container was dumped over with cans spread about. Suspecting that a bear might be in the area, he sent our guests down the path toward their cabin while he circled down toward the garbage bin to check things out. Suddenly, he heard something in the pine tree above him. Bill recalled, "I knew it wasn't a bird in the top of the tree!" The bear, spooked by the Suburban and the guests, had climbed up the tree to hide. Watching as the bear made its way down the tree, tearing branches as he descended, I'm not sure which one was more scared, the bear; the guests; or Shane and Brandon. The bear hit the ground, wide-eyed, head swinging from side to side. Shane and Brandon waddled down the path to the cabin, weighed down with the luggage strapped over them as the guests ran screaming and waving their arms overhead. It was quite a sight!

The black bear made a few more visits to our Ranch, once opening the hummingbird feeder and drinking the juice inside without breaking the feeder. Another time we found him sitting flat on his behind, his face buried in a can of grease, much like Winnie the Pooh and his jar of honey. And as we were told, once he discovered that there really was no food at our place that he could easily access, he would leave us alone.

Moose were plentiful in the Big Horns and became part of our everyday life at the Ranch. I must say, they became one of my favorite things about the Ranch. Although we shared our Ranch with the moose, we did so in a respectful way. We respected the fact that moose are wild animals and should be treated as such and *attempted* to instill this in our staff and guests.

Moose would graze on the grasses in the front pasture and eat off of the willows outlining the pastures. Grazing among the horses, the wranglers would often mistake the moose for the horses in the morning as they ran the horses into the paddock area.

The guests and staff thoroughly enjoyed experiencing the moose and photographing them. The dining room was enclosed in glass and looked out over the front pasture and beyond to the willows. It was not uncommon during dinner that someone would spot a moose which followed by guests grabbing their cameras to photograph it.

Tanja, a wrangler, found herself in a race with a moose one day as she was riding by herself. As she and her horse ran along a trail, a moose appeared next to her running alongside her horse. It was cute to hear her tell the story in her German accent and see the excitement in her face.

Bill and I were entertainment for a cow moose one morning as we were cleaning two separate cabins. The moose decided to hold us captive on the porch of our respective cabin. As soon as one of us would attempt to leave the porch, she would run over and chase us back. Back and forth she went for about an hour before she tired of the game and sauntered down the lane.

One evening Bill and I held a staff meeting down at the wranglers' quarters. As we ended our meeting, it was just getting dark. The whole group headed around the building and toward the lodge when someone yelled, "Watch out for the moose!" Bill and I were in front, John and Anne were behind us, and five other staff members were behind them. Bill and I immediately looked toward the willows, but didn't see anything. As we turned and looked toward the paddock area, the moose was coming over the fence and charging toward us with its head down. Chaos ensued as everyone was yelling and scattering. John and Anne fell down and there was nowhere for Bill and me to go. As the moose drew within feet of me and Bill, we could see his large spoons coming straight for us. Bill and I were holding hands and he claims that he was trying to push me out of the way. (My recollection is that it felt more like he was pulling me in front of him). Suddenly and from out of nowhere, Cali, our Alaskan Malamute, charged at the moose's feet, which diverted the moose away from us and toward her. The moose followed Cali down through the pasture. Cali was able to outrun the moose. We believe that Cali saved me and Bill from being badly hurt that day and Cali went from milk bones to T-bones that day. As a side note, our other dog Lucy had been walking with us but did not stick around for any heroics. She saw the moose and got out of Dodge.

Early one spring day we noticed a cow moose and her baby grazing on the hillside just behind the lodge. Oftentimes during the spring and summer this twosome would be spotted in the area of the Ranch. During the summer months the campers down near Shell Creek noticed that the cow moose had disappeared and the baby moose seemed to be on her own. Sharing their concern over the wellbeing of the baby moose with the forest ranger only brought the news that the common practice of the Forest Service is to "let nature take its course." The probability that a mountain lion would overtake the small moose concerned the campers to such a degree that they persisted in talking to the forest ranger about a possible solution. Eventually, one of the forest rangers put out an alert to zoos that are known for taking in such stray animals. The Columbus Zoo responded to the alert and came to the Big Horn Mountains to capture the small moose and place her in their zoo.

In the evenings, coyotes could be heard yipping and howling back and forth between the mountain ridges. One summer, a coyote seemed to adopt the Ranch and would show up every morning as the horses were saddled and prepared for the day. He hung around the paddock area, although keeping a safe distance; he seemed curious about the goings on and didn't seem threatened by the activity around the Ranch. He never came close enough to cause concern and disappeared as fall weather arrived.

Across the road, in front of and high above the Ranch, was an outcropping of rocks that earned the name of Eagles Nest years before our tenure at the Ranch. Early in the spring if you watched closely, you could see baby eagles learning how to fly from their nest for the first time.

Early in the fall the elk would move closer to the Ranch and could be heard bugling during the fall rut. Occasionally, we would catch a herd of twelve to fifteen elk as they marched single file across the ridge in front of the Ranch. The silhouette of the herd moving across the horizon was an awesome sight.

Signs of mountain lion were prevalent, but only on a rare occasion were they spotted. Bill, however, had a hair-raising experience one winter evening with a mountain lion. On Christmas Eve, the year I was in Ohio for the birth of our first grandchild, Bill drove the snowmobile up to the top of the mountain to call me on his cell phone. The phone at the Ranch (as was often the case) was not working. As we talked on the telephone, he heard a mountain lion screech. As he explained, it was way too close for comfort and he felt that it was stalking him. He decided that he should start the snowmobile and head back to the lodge. Unfortunately, I could not reach him for several days following that phone call and was relieved to hear from him when he finally called me several days later.

Mountain goats were often spotted in the spring at the entrance to Shell Canyon and Bill and I spotted a bobcat one evening in that same location. Danny, a winter staff member, and I captured a picture of the mountain goats and a bald eagle as it flew through the canyon one spring morning as we drove to Greybull. Wild turkeys and red fox are also plentiful and a common sight in the Big Horns and around the Ranch.

Porcupine were plentiful and a nuisance around the Ranch. On numerous occasions Bill spent hours pulling porcupine quills out of the dogs and horses. The dogs would attempt to bite at the porcupines, which left them with a mouth full of porcupine quills. The horses were inquisitive and in fulfilling their own curiosity, would nudge the strange little animal, leaving them with quills in their muzzle. Bill began saving the quills which numbered in the hundreds.

Beaver dams were also a usual sight on the mountain pass coming across the mountain from Sheridan on Highway 14.

Winter at the Ranch

Winter at the Ranch was a glorious time of the year. Although we had snow every month of the year, the heavy snow usually arrived in mid-October and lasted through mid-May. The snow blankets the mountains and can measure depths of 250 inches, covering the sage brush and, most often, the fences. The dry climate creates snow that is fluffy and shimmers in the bright sunlight like millions of tiny diamonds. The bright blue Wyoming skies and the sparkling snow provide an exquisite picture.

During the winter months, the road leading into the Ranch is part of a groomed snowmobile trail system that covers the entire mountain. The trails connect the lodges located at Burgess Junction, passing Antelope Butte Ski Resort, and continuing past our Ranch and Snowshoe Lodge, continuing over the mountain and ending at Meadowlark Lodge on the South side of the mountain. Snowmobilers flock to the Big Horn Mountains to enjoy the abundance of snow and the miles of groomed snowmobile trails.

The trail system on the mountain was groomed overnight. The groomer was a local guy that lived in Sheridan. Grooming was a lonely, cold, and dangerous job. The groomer moved very slowly over the trails and several sections of the trail were steep and dangerous. The groomer would oftentimes stop by our Ranch for a hot cup of coffee, a piece of pie, and a few minutes of conversation before continuing up over the top of the mountain. Everyone watched out for the groomer to ensure his safety. Martin, from Snowshoe Lodge, would wait up until late into the night until he could see the light from the groomers rig returning from his trip to the southern end of the trail system.

I especially enjoyed hearing the stories of the wildlife the groomer saw during his nighttime trips across the mountain. He spoke often of seeing mountain lion, bear, and moose during his nighttime adventure.

Christmas time on the mountain held a magical feeling. Bill and I would travel into the forest to locate the perfect fresh pine tree and pull it back to the Ranch behind the snowmobile. Even with the cathedral ceilings in the great room, the tree often had to be trimmed to fit beneath the top of the log ceiling.

Many of the lodges on the mountain gathered at Big Horn Mountain Lodge for the annual "Christmas on the Mountain" dinner. It was a great time of sharing good food, fellowship, and storytelling. The evening ended with the reading of the Christmas Story.

Our winter season started just before Christmas and ran through mid-April, or as long as the snow permitted. The end of February and the month of March were the busiest weeks during the snowmobile season. The snowfall during that time provided the snowmobilers their greatest riding experiences. Snowfall was deep and the trails were smooth.

Big Horn Safari was a family-owned business out of Sheridan who provided not only guided tours on the mountain, but also provided snowmobile rentals for those individuals not owning their own snowmobile. The Arzy Family and their guides were the nicest people and helped us immensely in learning about and building our winter business. The Arzy boys and their guides had grown up on the mountain and were familiar with the snowmobile business and were instrumental in expanding the trails and attracting visitors to the Big Horn Mountain in the winter months. Big Horn Safari would book groups into the Ranch and guide daily trips designed for the specific group. Whether it was a family or a group of adventure seeking guys, they were ready for the challenge. They were also capable of assisting snowmobilers with repairs on their own machines when the need arose.

The snowmobilers that were attracted to our Ranch were those that enjoyed a family atmosphere and weren't attracted to the bar scene. They might enjoy a cocktail after dinner, but partying all evening was not what they desired. They played hard all day and came back to the Ranch in the evening to enjoy a hearty dinner followed by relaxing in front of the TV or playing a hand of cards before retiring to their cabins.

Our snowmobilers most often came from Wisconsin, Minnesota, Illinois, and Iowa, but we had groups from many others states, as well. After a few years, our return business grew to around 80 percent. Although we had many families and couples stay at the Ranch during snowmobile season, the majority of our guests were groups of guys. And these guys loved to eat!

The guys typically ate a big breakfast, snowmobiled all day and returned in the evening for dinner. We served meals that were "meat and potato" kind of meals, roast beef, steak, and pork roast, to name a few. Along with homemade bread and rolls, homemade pies were also fast favorites of the guys. I quickly learned to have the recipes ready as the guys always requested them to take home to their wives.

One dark, winter evening, we were in the middle of serving dinner and we heard the sound of snowmobiles coming up the road and into the Ranch. All of our guests had previously returned from their day of playing on the mountain and we were not expecting anyone else, so we were curious who this could be. When the two snowmobilers came into the lodge, I was surprised and delighted when they announced that they had snowmobiled all the way across the mountain from the lodge at Burgess Junction after hearing about my delicious pies and were hoping that I had a piece of pie that they could purchase. Luckily, I had extra that night.

Our second winter season a group of guys from Wisconsin stayed at the Ranch. There were twelve in their group and we learned that Ron had played football for the Green Bay Packers. Ron was a big guy. He had to duck and turn sideways going through our doorways in the lodge. Dinner their first night was our usual meat and potato feast with all the trimmings served family style. When the group finished eating, there was nothing left. Not a scrap or crumb of anything left over. This caused me worry, as I did not want anyone to leave the table hungry. The next meal I served this group was breakfast the next morning and I doubled the amount of food that was served. When they left the table, once again, there was nothing left. After increasing the amount of food I served several times, with the same results, Bill finally told me, "Susie, I think you could put dirt in a dish and cover it with BBQ sauce and these guys would still eat it all up. They just like to eat." I listened to his advice and relaxed about the food portions. We are pretty sure we didn't make any money on this group of guys.

This same group of guys stayed with us year after year during snowmobile season. It pleased Bill and me that they felt at home at the Ranch and some days enjoyed spending the whole day at the lodge watching movies and hanging out.

During one of their visits to the Ranch, Ron came bursting through the door in the middle of the day exclaiming that Derek had crashed his snowmobile and was badly hurt. I immediately called 911 and explained to them that we needed emergency care up on the mountain. Between Ron, Bill, and a forest ranger that was at the Ranch at the time, they were able to pin-point where on the mountain the injured party was waiting. They immediately dispatched a life flight helicopter to Derek's location. It took two hours before the helicopter arrived to assist Derek, but during that time, the other guys kept him lying on the cold snow to relieve the pain. The helicopter finally arrived and the Emergency Medical Team assessed Derek's condition, determining that he had broken his back. When they loaded Derek into the helicopter and attempted to take off, they were unable to take off because the helicopter was too heavy. Because it was a clear day and at the high elevation, there was not enough air to create the lift needed to allow the helicopter to take off. They had to unload Derek and dump some fuel before once again attempting to take off. Fortunately, this time they were able to take off, but now they only had enough fuel to transport Derek to the airport in Sheridan. When they arrived in Sheridan, they transferred him to a plane which flew him to the larger hospital in Billings, Montana. It was confirmed that Derek had broken his back and after a lengthy surgery, he spent the next few weeks in the hospital in Billings before returning home to Wisconsin.

Derek was jumping his snowmobile off a two-story cliff at the time of the accident and, due to the low snowfall that winter, the impact upon landing was much too drastic and his back took the brunt of the impact. Derek fully recovered over a period of time and was back snowmobiling the next winter.

The Petersen Group was one of our winter groups that stayed at the Ranch year after year. They were from Minnesota and always came with a large entourage, usually fifteen to eighteen people in their group. The Petersen Group usually came around Christmas and stayed for four or five days. Jerry had two girls that were very close in age and Bill pulled them in a two seat cart behind his snowmobile down to the Suburban one day as they accompanied him to Shell to feed the horses. They looked adorable sitting in this little cart. Lucy was a puppy at the age of six weeks the first time the girls visited the Ranch and they loved to carry her around, much to Lucy's displeasure. It was good for Lucy to be around the girls as she learned to adapt to children quite quickly.

Among the regular visitors to the Ranch during the winter season were the Forest Service Security Officers. They were assigned to the mountain during the winter snowmobile season to check permits, assist in emergencies and to insure that snowmobilers didn't wander into the Wilderness Area. The Wilderness Area is a protected portion of the National Forest where motorized vehicles are not permitted.

We welcomed the security officers to the Ranch and shared many meals with them during their stay. They were great people and we enjoyed getting to know them and sharing stories of our families. Bill had the adventure of accompanying them on the trail system one day. He came home with many stories, but especially his thrill of riding with them at high speeds across the long stretches of the trail system.

Powder Magazine sent one of their writers and a photographer along with a couple other guys to stay with us during the winter and wrote a story about our

Ranch in their magazine. A couple of the guys in their group were extreme skiers—the ones you see on television that jump out of helicopters and ski down the side of the steep mountains. They had some exciting stories to tell about their adventures and the broken bones that accompanied this extreme sport.

Snowmobilers are like fishermen, they enjoy telling stories about their day's adventures. Many times as I listened to the stories, I heard them talk of "white out" conditions, but I never quite understood the ramifications of this snow condition. As is often true, I soon learned firsthand what a "white out" meant.

One winter day, the snowmobilers had eaten breakfast and left the Ranch for a day of playing in the snow. Bill and I decided to take a break and head over the mountain to Antelope Butte. Antelope Butte is the ski lodge that is about eight miles from our Ranch on a groomed snowmobile trail that cuts across the top of the mountain. It was snowing lightly as we travelled across the mountain to the ski lodge.

We arrived at the ski lodge and spent the next several hours visiting with Emerson, the owner of Antelope Butte, catching up on the latest news, the weather, and the latest gossip on the mountain. As we sat there, it began to snow harder. Eventually, we decided to head back to the Ranch. As we started to leave, Emerson suggested that if we had any trouble up on the top of the mountain we should come back and he would load our snowmobile in his truck and drive us around to the road that leads to the Ranch.

We left the ski lodge and headed up the groomed trail toward the top of the mountain. It had started snowing even harder now. The closer we got to the top of the mountain, the visibility became worse. Although the trails are well marked, the markers were becoming harder to locate. Not having experienced this before and remembering the horror stories from our snowmobilers (people driving off the edge of a cliff or driving off the groomed trail and burying the snowmobile in the deep snow), I began to panic. In my mind all I could hear was Emerson telling us to come back to the ski lodge. I now understood what a "white out" was. I could hardly see a few inches from my face.

Suddenly Bill stopped the sled. He couldn't locate the next marker. I could no longer control my panic and started to yell. "We need to turn around and go back! Please Bill – go back!"

Bill calmly stood up on the sled, turned toward me and grabbed my face saying, "Get a hold of yourself! I know what I am doing!"

Bill sat back down and drove the sled in a big circle, which brought us back to the next marker on the trail. As we continued down the trail visibility became clearer and we made our way safely back to the Ranch.

Later that evening as we told our story to our guests, they finished our story by telling us that they must have come through that same spot shortly after us and found themselves in the same predicament. They followed the tracks in the snow that made the big circle and found the next trail marker that led them back to the groomed trail.

Ray was a guide on the mountain during the winter season and would often stop by the Ranch with his group of snowmobilers for hot coffee and lunch. Ray was in his early seventies but remained healthy and sturdy for his age. He had lived in the area his whole life and knew the mountain like the back of his hand. His wife often came along and Ray had installed a tall flag on the back of her snowmobile so he could keep track of her during their treks across the mountain. Ray often called a few days ahead and made arrangements to bring a group of snowmobilers to the Ranch for an early breakfast before they headed down the southern end of the trail. We enjoyed talking to Ray, as he always knew the latest news on the mountain and was always eager to share. We appreciated the business he brought to us and another opportunity to market the Ranch.

Ray had everyone worried on one occasion when during a storm on the mountain he became separated from his group and was unable to climb out of a canyon with his snowmobile. Ray later told me of the cold night he spent in the canyon and how he built a fire to dry his clothes and keep warm during the cold winter night. It wasn't the first time Ray had spent the night in the elements over the years and it was interesting to hear of his many adventures.

Hauling groceries into the Ranch added to the winter adventure. Since our trucks were parked four miles away from the Ranch, we hooked a sled to the back of our snowmobile and drove the four miles to the truck. We then drove the thirty-one miles to Greybull, where we shopped for our groceries. Once the groceries where purchased they were loaded in the Suburban for the fifty minute drive back to the parking lot below the Ranch. The groceries were then loaded into the sled that was pulled behind the snowmobile up the winding road to the Ranch.

One day as I drove the snowmobile pulling the sled down the trail to the Suburban, something just didn't feel right. As I stopped the snowmobile, I realized that the sled was missing. I had no idea where it had separated and the horrible prospect of the sled sitting in the middle of the trail and the threat of the sled causing an accident prompted me to quickly turn around in search of it. I located the sled about half way up the trail and after hooking it back up continued on my way to the Suburban and my shopping trip.

A later experience with the snowmobile proved to be even more terrifying. One cold, dark night as Bill and I were returning to the Ranch after having dinner and picking up groceries in Greybull, our snowmobile caught fire. A pin-size hole in the fuel line caused fuel to spray on the motor which then erupted in flames as we drove up the road to the Ranch. Flames were shooting from under the hood of the snowmobile. Bill and I both dove off the snowmobile simultaneously scooping snow to throw on the flames. The fire was quickly dowsed.

In the below zero temperatures, we hastily gathered the groceries and began the walk into the Ranch. Walking into the Ranch, however, became more difficult than we had thought. It was so dark that we frequently stepped off the edge of the groomed trail and were buried in waist deep snow. It was comical as we tried to pull ourselves out of the fluffy snow. We even joked that we didn't need to be the strongest or fastest to keep from getting eaten by a mountain lion or bear that might be lurking in the trees, but only smarter than the other. Needless to say, we both made it back to the lodge without being eaten by a mountain lion and we kept our sense of humor through it all.

December was a cold, dark month on the mountain. The days were short with sunset as early as three o'clock in the afternoon. Oftentimes, during the first few weeks of December, we would seldom see anyone on the mountain. The remote location of the Ranch coupled with the snow depths deterred anyone from venturing in our direction. So, a knock on our door late one night startled both Bill and I as we sat watching a movie. The County Sheriff had managed, through the deep snow, to drive his cruiser up the road to the Ranch before burying it in the deep snow. He explained to Bill that a couple of teenagers were suspected to have driven their Geo Tracker up on the mountain earlier in the day and had not returned. After they pulled the cruiser out of the deep snow, he asked Bill to ride his snowmobile over the trail to the south in an effort to locate the teenagers.

Bill made the trek up and over the mountain for as far as he could go under the weather conditions. His original tracks were snow covered as he made the return trip to the Ranch with no sign of the teenagers. We were told a few days later that the teenagers were found the next day on a side road coming from the South and were cold but otherwise unharmed.

Snowfall during the winter months varied considerably and our winter business relied heavily upon snowfall. The snowmobilers didn't want to travel the distance to the Big Horns if the snowfall wasn't plentiful and fun to play in. Bill and I learned early on that the winter business was unpredictable and because of this we didn't always hire staff during the winter months.

Our first winter season Brandon was still with us and his friend from college, Wichita (Don), also worked for us. They both were a big help and also good company during those long winter months. They worked hard during the day clearing snow, breaking ice, and they also helped me in the kitchen. In the evening, they played cards with the guests and occasionally were able to break away from the Ranch and enjoy snowmobiling across the mountain.

In addition to our regular guests who stayed for long weekends or week long stays, we offered lunch to snowmobilers traveling across the mountain. Since Ranger Creek Guest Ranch had not previously been open during the winter months, this was another way for us to market our Ranch to the snowmobilers who were staying at the lodges at Burgess Junction. We served hot chili and chicken noodle soup, sloppy joe and pulled pork sandwiches, chips, and hot drinks. Word about our hot lunches spread quickly and it took all of us to keep up with the lunch crowd. During peak season, it was not unusual for us to have forty-five snowmobilers stop by during lunchtime for a hot meal and good conversation. Many of these snowmobilers became regular guests at our Ranch, not only during the winter months, but during the summer season as well. A few years later, we added gasoline tanks which drew more snowmobilers to our side of the mountain to play in the snow.

Our daughter, Missy, spent one winter season with us and I thoroughly enjoyed her company. Missy and I were always close and talked everyday while we lived in Ohio. With the uncertainty of our telephone system at the Ranch, talking to her every day was impossible. So spending an entire winter with her at the Ranch was a real treat for me and certainly made the long winter months pass by more quickly. Missy cleaned the cabins for me and helped me in the kitchen. We talked non-stop during the day and she was able to experience the winter snowmobile season first hand.

The only other time we hired winter staff was during the winter that I stayed in Ohio for the birth of our first grandchild, Emma. Bill hired Danny who was from England and had visited us during the previous summer season. Danny assisted Bill in clearing snow and caring for the needs of the guests and we both felt more at ease just having someone else there in case of an emergency. Danny had a funny sense of humor and I really enjoyed his company when I returned from Ohio later in the season.

Cali, our Alaskan Malamute loved the winter months. She would lay outside curled up in the snow with her tail covering her nose. She sometimes would lie there so long that the snow would completely cover her. Suddenly, you would see the snow moving and Cali would appear, shaking off the snow as she stood up.

Occasionally, when we took the dogs with us to town or to Ohio after the winter season, the dogs had to ride on the snowmobile down to the truck. Cali didn't mind riding on the snowmobile and would jump up on the seat in front of Bill. When we were met by another snowmobile on the trail, it appeared as though Cali was driving. Lucy, on the other hand was more timid and snuggled into my jacket during the four mile trek to the truck.

Hunting Season

Hunting season begins in mid-October for mule deer. The hunting season for elk is held in early November and after a few years hunting season was also opened for moose. At first, of course, I didn't know what to expect during hunting season. But I soon learned that hunting season was pretty easy and that the hunters were for the most part self-sufficient. The hunters would come to the Ranch in big groups. All they want is to get up early, real early, and eat a hot and hearty breakfast. We started cooking breakfast at 4:00 a.m. and after packing lunch for the hunters and cleaning up the breakfast dishes, we went back to bed for a couple of hours. Unless the hunters fulfilled their tag, they rarely returned to the Ranch until around 6:00 p.m. After a hot and plentiful dinner, they were exhausted and retired to their cabins. Most of our hunters were from out of state and were not accustomed to the high altitude. So, in addition to getting up early and spending the day walking the steep inclines around the Ranch, they were also dealing with the effects of the altitude.

The Ranch sits at an altitude of 8300 feet and is surrounded by hills and mountains at higher altitudes. Bill and I were accustomed to the altitude, but our guests, even those from surrounding towns were unaccustomed to the high altitude and suffered as a result. Shortness of breath, dizziness, and headaches were the usual symptoms. The hunters, especially, were affected by the altitude because they hiked the hills and mountains around the Ranch in pursuit of their prey. Bill passed by two hunters one season as he hiked up the steep hill, carrying a ladder, to reset our telephone system. The two hunters were amazed that he could climb so effortlessly and not be out of breath.

We had been warned, and heeded the warning, to keep our dogs inside during hunting season and to keep the remaining horses in the paddock area close to the Ranch. The hunters that stayed at our Ranch were seasoned hunters and respectful of their surroundings, but as with anything in life, there are always those who were not so respectful or professional about their hunting abilities. We heard of horror stories from the forest rangers about horses being mistaken for mule deer and dogs being shot by the hunters.

Although we understood the need to do so, we were disappointed when we heard that the forest service had opened a moose hunting season in the Big Horn Mountains. The moose were plentiful around the Ranch and one of our favorite aspects of living on the mountain. It was remarkable to experience the nature of the moose on a daily basis. Bill's disappointment was apparent one day as a local hunter came through the door of the lodge excitedly telling Bill that he had shot *our moose* out in front of the Ranch. At first Bill thought he said that he had shot *our dog*. Bill quickly exclaimed, "You shot what?" Although the hunter quickly clarified that he had shot a moose, I could see the disappointment in Bill's eyes and shared in his feeling of loss over the shooting of the moose. Bill had been a hunter in

Ohio and all of my brothers were hunters, but we both enjoyed the moose so much and, in some sense of the word, they became like pets to us. We enjoyed shooting them with our camera instead.

Our Guests

Bill and I often commented how blessed we were with the character of the guests that we were fortunate to accommodate at the Ranch. As is often the case, dealing with the general public can be difficult, but during our years of caring for guests, we were fortunate to only have three families/groups that we would characterize as difficult. The majority of the guests who came to the Ranch were fun loving, caring, and respectful people who we enjoyed spending our time with and with whom we enjoyed sharing the Ranch.

Our guests came from forty-one different states and eleven different countries which included: Australia, Belgium, Canada, England, France, Germany, Ireland, Italy, Norway, Spain, and Switzerland. They were from all walks of life. Some lived in big cities and some lived in rural areas. But when they came to the Ranch they were all on vacation and ready to have fun. For the most part, we saw them at their best.

In each of our cabins a journal was available if a guest wished to leave us a note at the end of their ranch vacation. These messages still remain such a blessing to each of us that shared the experience with them. We treasure the time spent with each of our guests and the memories made. We consider our lives enriched for having known them.

Here are just a few of those memories:

One Last Hoorah

Lisa Reuter, the Travel Writer for The Columbus Dispatch (and now a dear friend) visited Ranger Creek Guest Ranch during our second summer season. Following her visit, she wrote an excellent article which was published on the front page of the travel section. As a result of that article, we booked many guests from Ohio and Wisconsin. One of those guests was Harold.

We received a letter from Harold one day which stated, "I am an eighty-five-year-old man from Ohio who is interested in booking a two week pack trip in the Big Horn Mountains. I haven't ridden a horse in over twenty years. And, by the way, I have diabetes." Bill responded to Harold and suggested that he come to the Ranch, ride the trails around the Ranch for a few days to acclimate to the altitude and to evaluate his riding abilities and then they would talk about a pack trip. Harold quickly agreed to those suggestions and arrived at the Ranch a few weeks later.

We soon learned that Harold was one of those people who can be admired for his zest for life. He had packed a lot of extraordinary experiences into his eighty-five years, and he was not yet ready to slow down. The stories he shared about his experiences were fascinating and when he told his stories, he held everyone's full attention.

Harold had brought his diabetes testing apparatus with him and was concerned when his levels were high. Together we worked on menus and after a few days were able to get his levels under control.

Harold was a tall, thin man with long legs which enabled him to sit well in the saddle. After his first day in the saddle, however, he had difficulty climbing off the horse. But, he was out of bed bright and early the next morning and eager to ride again. By the third day, Harold was ready to plan his pack trip.

Bill had decided to send two wranglers on the pack trip with Harold. Bill, Shane, Erica, Harold, and I spent most of a day planning out every detail of the pack trip. Plans were made to leave the next morning and wind their way into the Cloud Peak Wilderness Area on horseback. The wilderness area is a designated area in the National Forest where only non-motorized travel is permitted. Cooking must be done over campfire and all food and gear must be packed in and packed back out, requiring an additional horse to carry the supplies. Maps were surveyed and trails marked, menus were prepared and food packed. Everything was readied and packed for the five day trip.

That evening Harold came to me in the lodge and said he wanted to write a check for the unpaid portion of his account with us. I told him that he could settle up with us after the pack trip and on the last day of his visit with us. To my surprise, Harold asked in a matter-of-fact tone, "What if I croak while I'm out there?" I chuckled, but quickly answered, "Harold that is not an option!"

I watched from the lodge as they rode out of the Ranch early the next morning. Erica, Shane, Harold, and the pack horse, one by one, rode across the front of the pasture and down the lane eventually disappearing from sight as they began their adventure up the mountain and into the wilderness area. The ride up the mountain and across unfamiliar trails led them past sparkling lakes and lush green meadows with views of snow-capped mountains in the distance. A multitude of wildlife was visible and abundant along the way.

Upon their return to the Ranch five days later, Harold was excited to share his adventure and was full of praise for Shane and Erica for fulfilling his dream. He was exhausted from the trip and spent most of the day resting up. His last night at the Ranch was line dancing night and Harold once again amazed the young staff with his dancing abilities.

Harold departed the Ranch the next morning with a feeling of accomplishment, but left behind a long lasting impression on everyone, staff and fellow guests alike. His zest for life and exuberance to share his adventures were remarkable. Harold touched our lives in a way that few others could match.

We recently learned that Harold passed away in 2010 at the age of ninety-four.

> "This was a great challenge for this eighty-five-year-old who had many, many horse pack experiences: south out of Cody; the Sawtooth Mountains of Idaho; the highest peaks in New Mexico; and northwest of Denver over twenty years ago. I wanted 'one last hurrah' and Bill and Sue, you made it possible. Your lodge and cabins are above average. And your hospitality unsurpassed. Scott was extraordinarily helpful on day rides. And when it came to the five day over-

night trip in the mountains as high as 9400 feet – I could not have done it without the attention and help of Shane and Erica. They went overboard to assist me in every way possible.

Bill—your Buffalo Bill Cody act was historically interesting and delightful to watch. Sue—your cooking was the greatest and your interest in my diabetic requirements was greatly appreciated. I doubt I will pass this way again, but many will hear what I have expressed above."

Mary & Bob

Mary and Bob are college professors from Little Rock, Arkansas. They had previously visited the Big Horn Mountains and came specifically to view and photograph moose.

When they arrived at the Ranch one fall afternoon, Bill took their bags and walked them to their cabin. As they walked down the path to their cabin, Bill casually mentioned that the outhouse was just up the hill behind their cabin When they reached their cabin and Mary opened the door, she immediately yelled and socked Bob on the arm. Noticing the delight on Bill's face that he had pulled one over on her, she explained that she remembered asking many questions about the Ranch and the accommodations, but she just couldn't remember asking if the cabins had indoor plumbing. When she opened the door and saw the bathroom, she was so relieved and her first reaction was to hit someone—-Bob just happened to be the one closest to her at the time.

Mary and Bob would start their morning with an early breakfast and then head out to explore the area in hunt of moose. They were pleasantly surprised after spotting thirty-six moose during their stay in the Big Horn Mountains that year.

> "We spent three nights and two days here in Bill & Suzie's heaven. Came to see moose—saw thirty-six, twenty-eight of them bulls! We will take home many photos and many memories and we will return! More than all of the above, we have found new friends (Bill & Suzie and their kids). It is so comforting to know that America is alive and healthy up here in these mountains and Bill and Suzie are responsible for most of that feeling! God Bless you and everyone who took such good care of us."

The Corporate Group

Oftentimes and especially during our first few years at the Ranch, people would stop by to check out our facilities and see what improvements we had made. Many times this led to future bookings and we welcomed the opportunity to show off the improvements, hand out brochures, and talk about the programs and activities available to guests.

Early one summer afternoon, Harold and his wife, Pat, drove into the Ranch on a small motor bike. During our conversation, I learned that Harold had grown up in the area and, although he had moved away, many of his family still remained close by. Harold owned one of the summer cabins along Shell Creek and returned several times during the summer months to visit family and to fish and hike in the Big Horn Mountains. Harold and Pat were incredibly friendly and they were very familiar with the history and previous owners of the Ranch, which they freely shared with me during their visit. Harold and Pat were pleasantly surprised and delighted as I showed them around the Ranch and they could see the vast improvements we had made. Before they left, Harold commented that he had always wanted to bring the corporate staff of his company to the Big Horn Mountains for a retreat, but had never felt comfortable with any of the establishments available on the mountain. He inquired if I felt we could accommodate a corporate retreat at Ranger Creek Guest Ranch. I assured him that I felt confident that we could accommodate them and he said he would have someone call me to talk about the details.

The very next week I received a call from Dee, a member of Harold's staff, to discuss the details of scheduling a corporate retreat at our Ranch. Dee and I talked about the number of people we could accommodate, the schedule for the retreat and timing of their meetings, activities available during their free time, and dates for their visit.

During my conversation with Dee, I learned that Harold was the President and CEO of a Fortune 500 Company that was headquartered out of Arkansas. Part of the company operations were also in Texas. The group that was scheduled to come to the Ranch included the top executives of this company. The week before the group was scheduled to arrive at the Ranch,

Dee called and asked me to arrange for the rental of three SUVs which were to be waiting for them at the local airport in Greybull. Dee also wanted to talk about the food for the retreat. He asked about the menu and made several suggestions. He said that if I served steak, Harold wanted the best steaks. Harold would be happy with my meat and potato meals, just top notch cuts of meat and plenty of everything. Dee stressed that they were willing to pay the extra cost for the food, they just wanted the very best for their top executives.

Both Harold and Dee were so friendly and very easy going, but as the date drew close for our first corporate retreat, my nerves took over. Sleepless nights and worrisome days prevailed as I prepared for the upcoming retreat. Corporate retreats were part of our plan for the Ranch, but preparing for the *first* retreat was frightening and self-doubt seemed to take control. I had nightmares about the preparation of the food and visions of something going wrong.

The group landed their corporate jet at the local airport on Wednesday afternoon. After loading the SUVs with their luggage and meeting materials, they made a stop at the local grocery store loading up on snacks and beverages and also stopped for lunch in Greybull before heading up the mountain to the Ranch. Upon their arrival at the Ranch, there was a flurry of activity as we assigned cabins, stored the beverages and answered questions about the Ranch and the area. I chuckled as the guys unloaded their snacks onto the table in the great room. They had purchased every kind of snack imaginable and the snacks consumed the entire table.

Eager to relax and enjoy the Big Horn Mountains, a few of the guys headed out to do some fishing. A couple of the guys enjoyed taking a trail ride around the Ranch, while others decided to relax, prop their feet up, and enjoy the view from the front porch of the lodge.

The whole group returned to the lodge for dinner and this is when we really started to get to know these guys. We quickly learned that although they were hard working professionals, they were also fun loving, genuine guys who knew how to kick back and enjoy their surroundings. And, although they weren't shy in asking for what they wanted, they were quick to acknowledge and praise the hard work and effort it took to provide for their needs.

The next few days, they were up early, ate breakfast, and began their business meetings in the Great Room, pausing only for lunch and a few short breaks. Late in the afternoon, they adjourned their meeting and headed out to do some fishing and horseback riding.

My nervousness over meeting their needs had all but subsided until dinner on the third day. Bill was preparing to grill chicken on the outside grill. Shortly after lighting the grill, the glass front of the grill exploded, sending glass flying everywhere. Thankfully, we had not yet placed the chicken on the grill. We quickly brought the chicken inside and cooked it on the stove. One of the guests had noticed what was happening and asked a few questions. We felt fortunate that we had averted a disaster and didn't give it another thought.

Shortly before the Corporate Group left the Ranch to return home, Dee came to me and inquired regarding the best way to send something to us here at the Ranch. I was thinking maybe they wanted to send us a framed picture, as many of our previous guests had sent us enlarged, framed pictures of Bill and I or of the scenery around the Ranch. When I told him that UPS delivers packages to the Ranch, he pressed with: "What if it is something large?" I tried to answer his question, but it didn't seem as though I was giving him the answer that satisfied his question.

A few weeks later, a large semi-truck drove up the lane and parked near the Lodge. As this was not a usual sight to see this far up on this mountain road, I met him half way between the truck and the lodge. Carrying a handful of papers, he announced that he was delivering my stove. He was not happy when I told him that I had not ordered a stove. I'm sure he was thinking, *I drove this huge truck all the way up this narrow mountain road and now this lady says she didn't order a stove.* Annoyed by the thought, he handed me the paperwork and I quickly realized that it wasn't a stove, it was a grill and it had been sent by the Corporate Group. The Corporate Group had replaced our damaged grill with a huge, beautiful new grill. I was speechless!

The Corporate Group held their corporate retreat each of the following years that we remained at the Ranch. Bill and I and the staff looked forward to their return each year with such excitement. These guys became good friends and a few especially enjoyed playing tricks on me. They loved to hear me shriek when I found fish heads in my dish water. Kerly especially caught me off guard one day as I was busy working in the kitchen.

When he returned from riding horses with Billy, our wrangler, Kerly acted very serious as he inquired about our policy of matching horses with riders. As I was explaining the premise behind the policy and how we liked to match the horse that most likely resembles the rider in nature and ability, I noticed that he and Billy started getting this ornery look on their face. I must admit I didn't catch on until I asked the question that they were waiting to hear, "Which horse did you ride?" To which Kerly proudly answered, "Thurston!" You see, Thurston was well endowed. The guys were delighted when my face turned bright red.

The practical joke went back and forth between the staff and the Corporate Group. When the guys brought their fish back to the Ranch, they would clean them, place them in plastic bags, and put them in the freezer. Dee had caught a large bass and was showing it off to everyone before placing it in the freezer. He was so proud of his prize catch. Bill later switched his fish with a small fish in the freezer, causing Dee a moment of panic when he went to retrieve it from the freezer. Bill tried to convince him that his fish had shrunk, but he didn't buy the story.

Whenever Harold had the opportunity, he referred people to our Ranch and each year during his own family reunion would use the Ranch as overflow for out-of-town family and friends. Dee came one year and brought his son; and Brad, the company pilot, also stayed with us several times. I fondly remember one evening when Brad, Dee, and Jim, my brother-in-law, were line dancing with the other guests in the Great

Room. The three of them kept us in stitches as they attempted to learn the steps to the dance. Jim danced out one door of the Great Room and back in the other without missing a beat.

Harold commented with great sentiment in his voice as he stood in the Great Room of the Lodge during the last year the Corporate Group visited the Ranch, that most of the important decisions regarding their company had been made right here in this room.

> "You all are such great, genuine, nice people.
> I have truly enjoyed my stay and am already
> planning a return trip w/my family. Thank you
> so much for your warm hospitality. I wish you
> all that which you deserve – the best. Until next
> time, my thoughts and prayers are with you."

The Reunion Group

With its wholesome nature, its proximity to Yellowstone National Park and activities that kept guests of all ages entertained, the Ranch provided the perfect setting for a family reunion.

We had many reunion groups stay at the Ranch; however, our first reunion group that booked the entire Ranch still holds special memories. The group consisted of ten adults and eight children ranging in age from three to eighty-five: grandma and grandpa; two daughters; a granddaughter, a grandson, and their spouses; a younger grandson and granddaughter; and six great-grandchildren.

Grandma and Grandpa lived in New Hampshire and most of the family remained in that area. Ginny, the daughter, and her husband had moved to Alexandria, Virginia, with their jobs. Ginny had organized the vacation and corresponded with Bill and me for about a year before their arrival to the Ranch. It was touching to hear that one of the young couples was struggling to meet their portion of the cost of the trip and that the other members of the family had throughout the year chipped in as birthday and Christmas gifts helping them meet the expenses.

We had rented a van to pick the group up from the airport and also for their trip to Cody. Upon their arrival at the Ranch, similar in nature to most families that we had met, it was immediately obvious who got along with whom and the nature of their family dynamics. A few times during the week the family game time ended in loud voices and abrupt endings.

The core group enjoyed trail riding and participated in every trail ride available during their week at the Ranch. Five-year-old Josh rode each and every ride during their stay, even the Ridge Ride. Three-year-old Karen and three-and-a-half-year-old Jarod were satisfied with their daily trail ride through the pasture led by Wild Bill or Children's Wrangler Jess. They were so cute outfitted in their cowboy hats and boots. Wild Bill coaxed Jarod to tip his hat and say, "Hey, Good Lookin," as they passed by the front of the lodge. His ornery grin evidenced his willingness to obey. Even Grandpa sat on a horse for a group picture marking their ranch vacation.

Ginny's husband Bill had set up his laptop in the dining room of the lodge, commenting that he wasn't interested in trail riding, and would be spending most of his time right there in the dining room working. His suggestions for the Ranch included TVs in the cabins and a screened in porch on the front of the lodge. After coaxing from his wife and children, he agreed to join them for a trail ride and quickly became enamored with the beauty of the Big Horn Mountains. Bill joined the group for the remainder of the trail rides and talked endlessly of the wildlife and magnificent scenery he had witnessed during each ride. Shortly before their departure from the Ranch, Bill pulled Wild Bill and me aside and told us "not to change a thing" and that he had thoroughly enjoyed his visit to the Ranch. He explained that it was a welcome and relaxed respite from his busy life back home.

> "Thanks for making our family reunion such a memorable experience. Everyone from three to eighty-five had a wonderful time. Billy will never forget his eighth birthday! The food was wonderful and the riding was terrific. I won't be able to describe the views, they were breathtaking. You all did so much to make our visit enjoyable. I can't say one thing was the 'best', because it all was! We look forward to our next trip."

Dale and Steph

The northern state of Minnesota averages fifty-five inches of snow each year and snowmobiling is one of the favorite sports of most Minnesotans. When they aren't snowmobiling at home, they enjoy traveling to the West to experience snowmobiling in the mountains. Bill and I attended a vacation convention in Minneapolis each year to market the Ranch. During the four day show, Bill liked to roam around and talk to the various vendors, making contacts in the business, and checking out the array of equipment available at the show. During one of the shows, he talked with a vendor that sold cargo sleds that are pulled behind a snowmobile. We desperately needed a cargo sled for the winter business and during the four-day vacation show Dale and Bill came to an agreement on one of the sleds. In exchange for part of the cost of the sled, Bill traded a vacation at the Ranch during the summer season.

Dale and his wife, Steph, were a young couple from Albuquerque, New Mexico. Their experience riding horses was minimal and naturally they were quite nervous, but extremely excited when it came time to climb upon their assigned horse. As was the usual practice, the wrangler gave a short safety talk and then helped Dale and Steph up on their horse. Dale was so excited that he literally hyperventilated. Wild Bill and Shane worked with Dale and Steph in the pasture area for a while before moving on to the orientation trail for a short ride. As Dale and Steph started settling into the saddle and feeling more comfortable on their horse, they calmed down and really started enjoying their Ranch experience.

They both were eager to help out in the paddock with the horses and were often comical to watch as they learned many aspects of working with the horses. One evening, Wild Bill and Shane were running some horses into the paddock area and asked Dale to open and close the gate for them as they ran the horses in. I was in the paddock area and had to smile as I noticed Dale opening and quickly closing the gate several times as he waited for the horses to arrive. Dale took his job very seriously and was *practicing* opening and closing the gate so he would be sure to do it right when the time came.

Dale and Steph are an example of guests that made our experience at the Ranch so rewarding. They freely admitted that they would not have been able to afford a Ranch vacation, but they appreciated their experience probably more than anyone else who visited the Ranch. They were truly grateful for the experience and would not soon forget their vacation at Ranger Creek Guest Ranch.

> "What can we say?! This trip was more than we could have ever imagined! We are so fortunate to have been your guests here for an entire week. From the scenery to every last detail in the cabin, everything was wonderful. All your wranglers made us feel that we were old friends who had stopped by for a visit. Sue, you made us feel so welcome with your smile and hospitality. The food was excellent and the cabins were most comfortable. Bill, giving us the freedom to run with the horses was unbelievable...we will never forget it. Thank you all so much for truly making this the best time in our lives. Hope to be with you again here at Ranger Creek."

Swiss Contingent

We called them the Swiss Contingent, six adults and twelve children from Switzerland. The three men were attorneys and were, at the time, the President, the Past President, and the Future President of the Bar Association in Geneva, Switzerland. Alex and his family had stayed at our Ranch the previous summer and had invited their friends to join them on their return trip to the Ranch. All six adults spoke fluent English, but only the oldest of the children either understood or spoke any English. Although communicating was sometimes challenging, we soon learned that laughter is a universal language. The children ranged in ages from six to twelve. When they weren't riding horses, they enjoyed marching around the Ranch chanting their favorite song.

Little Elsa was a good little rider but was caught off guard one day when her horse, Crow, took off with her. Wild Bill was able to catch up with the wide-eyed rider and gain control of her horse. Although a little apprehensive, Elsa continued riding Crow throughout the remainder of her vacation.

Wild Bill accompanied Alec, Beneit, and Pierre on an all-day ride to Shell Reservoir. The weather that day, which is often the case in the mountains, changed as they climbed higher up the mountain. The typical warm and sunny August weather changed into rain and eventually snowflakes during their ride that took them into the higher elevations.

"When arriving here we were thinking that we knew about riding in the mountains, because we do that a lot back in the Swiss Alps. Your horses taught us much more than we ever knew! And you Bill, Sue, family, and wranglers taught us about hospitality and kindness for which we do thank you very much. We return home with a full load of beautiful and happy times!"

Merry, Tom, & Devon

Devon was ten when she and her Mom talked Tom into visiting the Ranch for the first time. Devon and Merry were avid riders in their hometown of Waukesha, Wisconsin. Devon was a tiny, quiet little girl who could handle a horse as well as most of our wranglers. She and Merry were excited about riding horses in the mountains, but Tom had planned to relax on the front porch with a good book. With Devon and Merry coaxing him, Tom agreed to join the trail rides, enjoying the company and the scenery along with the other guests.

Devon, Merry, and Tom vacationed at the Ranch year after year and we enjoyed watching Devon grow up. Although her plans to work on the Ranch as a wrangler didn't materialize due to the sale of the Ranch, she currently remains involved in training and working with horses and it has been our pleasure to stay connected with this wonderful family.

"I should be upset with you. This was supposed to be Merry & Devon's riding vacation and all I had to do was sit, relax, and read a couple of books. Instead, I rode, laughed, got

sore, and enjoyed the company and hospitality. I may never become a horseman, but I will
always have the great memories (and those two
books since I only got to read a few chapters).
Merry and Devon are already working on me to
come out again (I'm known as a soft touch). So,
I hope we will all meet again soon."

"I had the greatest time! Sorry we couldn't
stay for a week. I wish I were old enough to
wrangle here. Thanks for letting me round up
all the loose horses. The trail rides were awesome like usual. And, guess what, this was the
first time here I didn't get sore! I'm hoping to
see everyone again sometime. After four years,
I call this place home."

The Advil Gang

The notorious Advil Gang was made up of Mike,
Joanie, and Katie from Wisconsin; George and Nancy
from Ohio; Mary and Barb from Ohio; Amy and Mary
from South Carolina; Rick from Illinois; and Marlene,
Jim, and Justin (my sister, brother-in-law, and nephew)
from Ohio. Although they were more experienced riders than most of our guests, the type of riding and the
terrain surrounding the Ranch was challenging at times
and left them with sore muscles, prompting the need to
pop a few Advil upon their return to the Ranch.

Joanie wrote: "Thanks for the memories. This
was truly a great vacation! Everything from the
riding to the scenery, hospitality, friendships,
entertainment and food—it was all wonder-

ful. I felt like a part of a small family with our group—The Advil Gang. This certainly was relaxing and we had a lot of laughs. Good luck and hopefully we'll be back again. Thanks also to Bubba, Norway, and Barbell. As we ride off into the sunset..."

Suzi and Stephanie

Suzi and Stephanie were sisters from Germany. They visited the Ranch several years during the summer season. Stephanie's husband owned a restaurant in Germany and he adopted my recipe for Chocolate Chip Marsh Mellow Bars as a regular item on his menu. Much to my delight, Stephanie asked me to show her how to make a pumpkin pie during one of her visits to the Ranch. After we overcame the different methods of measuring between the two countries, we successfully prepared a pumpkin pie together.

Both Suzi and Stephanie were avid riders and fit right in with the other guests during their visit. Suzi is a gifted artist and we still enjoy many of her drawings in our cabin guest books.

> "We've got another wonderful stay at a wonderful place with you and made friends again. It has been so much fun—even got the chance chasing some cattle!! Yihaw! Thank you so much for showing me how to make a really delicious Pumpkin Pie, Sue. Next time we'll bring Johanna along! We both wish you the best and hope you'll send us pictures as grandparents, soon."

Wrangler Rick

Rick visited the Ranch our very first summer season. He was from Illinois and owned two horses of his own. Since he was comfortable in the saddle and knew his way around the corral, he quickly fit in with the wranglers. In fact, many of the other guests thought he was part of the staff. It was not uncommon to see him helping to clear the evening dishes from the table or throwing hay to the horses with the other staff. Rick would generally stay two weeks at the Ranch and we enjoyed his visits each and every year.

Bill and I were not surprised when Rick called us to tell us he was working as the head wrangler at Ranger Creek Guest Ranch for the new owners.

> "It's been a great week. You all have made me feel like family. Thank you for letting me be that. You will see me again. Good luck and God Bless."

Our First Guests

Our first official guests were our good friends, Gary and Elaine and their two daughters, Leslie and Reagan, from Ohio. Gary and Elaine are definitely "City Slickers" but were good sports in serving as guinea pigs in our efforts to work out the bugs in our program.

It was great to see Gary, Elaine, Leslie, and Reagan, as we had been working non-stop since our arrival in April and it was great to have an opportunity to relax for a few days with good friends and show off the results of our hard work. As a matter of fact, the plumber was just finishing up his work in the cabins and literally flushing the toilet in their cabin for the first time as Gary and Elaine drove up the lane and into the Ranch.

Matching them with a horse was an easy task as we had thirty horses to choose from. Teaching them to ride proved to be a little more difficult. Gary's horse stumbled during a daily ride and Gary landed on the ground. A cowboy he is not, but he had lots of good stories to tell upon returning home to Ohio. But once again, this gave us the opportunity to try out the trails and plan our riding program to start our summer season.

Aunt Anne, Uncle Ivan, Cousins Pat, Jack, & Amy

Bill's Aunt Anne, Uncle Ivan, cousins Pat, Jack, and Amy also visited the Ranch our first summer season. Uncle Ivan was eighty years old and had always dreamed of riding a horse in the West. Uncle Ivan rode every trail ride during his visit and thoroughly enjoyed himself, fulfilling one of his boyhood dreams.

Bill had specifically chosen Aunt Anne's horse for her as this was her first ride on a horse and she was understandably a little anxious and fearful about the experience. Bill had chosen Molly for Anne and had explained to Anne that Molly was partially blind and a very mild horse. Unfortunately, the explanation caused Anne more anxiety because she thought she needed to guide Molly around every pebble and branch that lay in her path. Anne nearly hyperventilated during her first ride. After further guidance from Bill and gentle coaching from Wrangler Kayleen, Anne relaxed and really enjoyed her remaining trail rides.

Amy especially enjoyed Peanut singing the song "Amy" especially for her around the campfire on her last evening at the Ranch.

Sharing this week with Anne, Ivan, Patty, Jack, and Amy was especially fulfilling for Bill and me. The Ranch and its quiet peaceful nature seemed to lend itself to those times of capturing relationships and making memories especially with those family members with whom we don't often have an opportunity to spend significant time.

> "It surely has been a fun experience being here this week. I would never have believed that I would ride a horse for the first time at seventy-five years and Ivan ride twice a day at nearly eighty. If you hadn't pursued your dream, Ivan and Pat would never have fulfilled their dream. We love you dearly and wish you only the best and may all your dreams come true. May all your future guests be as happy and have as much fun as we have."

Linda, Nate, McLain, & Evan

Linda, Nate, McLain, and Evan visited us from Ohio and although we hadn't previously met, were from the same area where we previously lived. Evan was about eight and really enjoyed Shane. Before they left the Ranch, he asked his Mom if they could take Shane home with them. McLain enjoyed dancing with Zack and Nate wanted to return to the Ranch as a wrangler someday. Linda wrote upon her return to Ohio that she really missed Wyoming. She wrote, "A friend of mine told me it takes about eight months to get over eight days in Wyoming. We've only been home one month and I'm still dying to go back."

> "We had the VERY BEST TIME here at Ranger Creek Ranch. We loved the horses, we loved the dogs, we loved the cabin, we loved the food...but...we especially loved getting to know the wonderful people who work here. We wish everyone here the best of health and the best of luck. We hope to come back someday very soon."

Myrella & Ken

Myrella and Ken were from New York City and worked for the Smithsonian Institution of American Art Museum. At the time, they were on assignment at the Dinosaur Digs in Shell and happened across the Ranch one weekend as they were exploring the Big Horn Mountains. During their weekend stay at the Ranch, it was fun seeing Myrella rolling around in the grass with our dogs, Cali and Layla. As one can imagine, their life in New York City was much different than that experienced at the Ranch. It was refreshing as Myrella openly expressed her wonder and enjoyment of the natural beauty and simple pleasures that the Ranch provided her. She provided a reminder of those things that could easily have been taken for granted.

"Although our stay was by necessity brief, it was nevertheless enchanting. We look forward to receiving your warm hospitality next summer."

Gill & Ruth

Gill and her daughter, Ruth, are from England. They came to the Ranch in the fall to ride horses and do a little shopping in Cody. Gill was about my own age and had such a great sense of humor. I really enjoyed her. Gill's visit was during a time when I was extremely homesick for Ohio and my family. We sat in the dining room for hours sharing stories and laughing just like old friends and at the time she was just what I needed.

The first night of their visit, we experienced a severe lightning storm. Lightning storms at the Ranch are unlike ordinary lightning storms. With the location of the Ranch sitting at altitudes of 8,300 feet, you feel as though you are directly in the middle of the storm. Gill was quick to proclaim the next morning that both she and Ruth were certain that everyone at the Ranch had expired as a result of the storm and they would awake to find complete destruction around them. Much to their delight and relief, they awoke the next morning to a beautiful fall day on the mountain and the staff still intact.

"Our very first experience of Western hospitality surpassed all our expectations. We've had a wonderful week riding in the most breathtaking scenery—and grateful thanks to you all for a most memorable holiday. Kindest regards to you all."

Ray & Pat

Ray and Pat visited the Ranch in celebration of their fortieth wedding anniversary. They commented one morning that they couldn't sleep. When we asked why they were having trouble sleeping, they commented, "It's too quiet!"

> "We're certainly glad we chose coming to Ranger Creek Ranch instead of a cruise for our fortieth anniversary. We were apprehensive, but the hospitality and warmth was great. The wranglers were perfect—great fun. Thanks Bill & Sue."

The Wohrer Family

The Wohrer Family visited the Ranch while on vacation in the United States from Paris, France. Philip enjoyed playing the guitar and singing on the front porch of the lodge with other guests. He was so embarrassed when he came to me during their stay to say that he was horsing around and broke a window in the cabin. He said that he couldn't even blame it on the kids, because he was the one that broke it. I told him that no harm was done and we quickly replaced the window.

> "It will certainly be the best memory of our trip in your country. Very difficult to go away after such enjoyment here. Thank you so much!"

The California Family

Vacationing in the mountains proved to be an experience for this California family when they experienced snow during their visit at the end of June. Although you can get snow at any time on the mountain, it was our first experience with several inches of snow at the end of June. The two boys, ages approximately five and six, were delighted about the snow, but mom and dad were somewhat nervous. They even contemplated leaving for fear of getting "snowed in." We tried to calm their fears pointing out that, although there was probably an inch or two on the ground, you could still see the grass through the snow. At the end of the week when they were getting ready to leave for home, they stated that they were so happy that they didn't leave and that they had a wonderful time.

> "Thank you for our great stay at your ranch. We know that the weather was a challenge during our stay (rain, hail, snow, snow, snow) but y'all made our visit very enjoyable regardless. Our boys liked the crafts, especially Will. And Jay now wants to come work for you as a wrangler when he turns sixteen. Thank you also for the great food and evening fun. We wish the very best to your wonderful family."

Warren

Warren was originally from Minnesota and first came to the Ranch as a guest with a group of snowmobilers. Warren shared our love of Big Ten football and basketball and we talked about our favorite teams, his Minnesota and ours, of course, Ohio State. Warren returned to the Ranch nearly every year either in the summer season or in the winter season. One year he brought his son along and rode horses and one year he brought his wife. Warren even showed up one year unexpectedly on his motorcycle joking that he was in the area and just happened to stop by. We always enjoyed sharing the Ranch with Warren and enjoyed his soft spoken, friendly nature.

> "What a beautiful spot you have here in the mountains – so glad my husband got me out here after having been here several times without me. I must say it is really something waking up to such beautiful scenery (not to mention horses peeking in the window). We thoroughly enjoyed our three days here. You make it easy to feel comfortable here. Thanks for everything!"

The Chicago Group

The Chicago group with twenty-eight guests was the largest single group that stayed at the Ranch for a week. Bill and I had corresponded with this group for about a year before their arrival. Gorge, the organizer of the group, was looking for a Ranch that could accommodate the entire group and yet only accommodate their group. As was the standard when a group insisted on booking the entire ranch, they tended to require us to also accommodate their schedule.

Generally, when a group required us to accommodate their schedule, the entire group abided by their schedule. This group was the exception. The bulk of the group would arrive late for breakfast and the remainder of the group straggled in over the next hour or so. The kitchen staff worked continuously preparing meals, keeping meals hot, cleaning up after the meals, and starting all over again. Because the meals started late, the trail rides also started late. The wranglers would saddle the horses and the rides would not even leave the Ranch until hours later as riders straggled in and out of the paddock area. I must admit though, the line of twenty-five or so horses plus the wranglers leaving the Ranch once the trail ride finally did leave was an awesome sight.

Although accommodating the group's schedule or lack thereof was difficult, I admired the closeness of this group. The group was a very family oriented group and between rides they played ball together as a family in front of the lodge. Many evenings as our day came to a close their entire group still remained around the campfire.

September 11, 2001

September 11, 2001, remains one of those dates when a person remembers where they were and what they were doing.

We had two couples from Ohio, a guest from Spain, and Bill's cousin from South Carolina at the Ranch on that day. It was Tuesday and Missy and I were in the kitchen preparing the food for the breakfast ride that morning. Bill, the wranglers, and guests were gathering in the paddock area to begin the morning ride. Erica came busting into the kitchen telling me to turn on the television as she nervously told me the news that she had heard on the radio. Missy, Erica, and I watched in astonishment as the commentator relayed the news of the terrorist attack on the twin towers in New York City.

Upon completion of the breakfast ride, everyone gathered in the great room to watch the unbelievable details as they unfolded throughout the morning. Each person anxiously awaited news from the various areas that were under attack. Since our telephones originated through cellular service, no connection was available. Bill drove a few of the guests off the mountain to make phone calls to family and loved ones.

Freddie, our guest from Spain, was scheduled to fly out of Sheridan on Saturday. When we arrived at the airport that morning, the new safety procedures created in response to the terrorist attacks caused the relocation of the parking lot well beyond the parameters of the airport building. As we expected, Freddie's international flight was delayed and he spent the next four days attempting to obtain a flight home.

How quickly things had changed. The week prior to the attacks, Bill and I drove to Cody to pick his cousin up at the small airport. When we arrived, we noticed a lot of traffic around the airport. We drove on into the airport and parked within a few feet from the front door. As we were getting out of our car, we noticed three black SUVs driving past us. Vice-President Dick Cheney was hanging out of the window waving to us and the other on-lookers. He had flown in to Cody to attend a birthday party for his friend who lived near the North Fork of the Yellowstone River. One week later as a result of the terrorist attacks the parking area was relocated across the highway.

Life on the Ranch

Bill and I both feel that it was a privilege to have owned and lived on the Ranch and we feel so richly blessed to have been given this experience. Our life while owning Ranger Creek Guest Ranch was so unlike our life while living in Ohio. And, although we loved our life in Ohio while growing up and especially while raising our own children, our lives in Wyoming were unique in many ways.

We had three guest seasons at the Ranch: Summer Season, Hunting Season, and Snowmobile Season. Between those seasons, we took advantage of the time and explored the Big Horn Mountains and visited other lodges and places on and near the mountain.

Snowshoe Lodge was our closest neighbor, located just above our Ranch on Paintrock Road. The Maylands owned Snowshoe Lodge and approximately 1700 acres of land around the lodge. The majority of land in the Big Horn Mountains is owned by the government and managed by the Forest Service. The Mayland family had settled on the property now known as Showshoe Lodge before the government made the land surrounding their land a National Forest.

The Maylands were quick to introduce themselves and helped to make us feel welcome to the mountain. We shared dinner together on occasion and they introduced us to their local friends and family. The Maylands lived in Shell and opened Snowshoe lodge to guests in the winter during snowmobile season and on rare occasions throughout the rest of the year.

Paintrock Lodge was another Lodge located at the end of Paintrock Road, approximately eighteen miles from our Ranch. The road leading up to this lodge was rough and washed out in various places along the route. Paintrock Lodge was only open three months during the summer and also during hunting season. The Lodge overlooked a large crystal clear lake. Bill and I drove up to introduce ourselves and meet the owners of this unique business. Paintrock Lodge was a small family owned lodge where guests came to ride horses, fish, and hunt and had been in business for over thirty years. The only way to learn about this lodge was "word of mouth." The owners did not advertise and did not even have a telephone at the lodge. Their only form of communication was a two-way radio system. Yet, their short season was completely booked months in advance. The owners of this lodge also lived off the mountain and ran the business from their home. In our world of internet and constant communication, it was refreshing to visit this unique lodge and meet the friendly, down to earth people who owned and ran this business and to see how if flourished in today's world.

While our friend Tom Sharpe was visiting, we took a drive around the area of Shell, which lay at the base of the mountain. Bill and Tom decided to explore a road that on the map appeared to travel up the mountain ending near our Ranch. The road, which looked more like a cow path, weaved through the foothills and then began a steep decent up the mountain. At times, the road was on sheer rock with a sharp drop off on one side. At one point, the path was so narrow that Tom got out of the truck looking to see how much solid ground Bill had available to maneuver the truck. I was not calmed by the fact that Tom held up both hands with his fingers indicating what looked like two to three inches on both sides and saying, "You have plenty of room!" When the truck started sliding backwards, I decided to walk. I got out of the truck and walked three times during the drive. As we crested the top of the mountain, the road turned into a cow path again, with grass growing in the middle as it twisted through cow pasture. Eventually, and after an hour and a half drive, the road ended up at Snowshoe Lodge, just above our Ranch. After thanking God that we made it home safely, I decided to let the guys go exploring on their own the next time.

During the summer season, Bill and I rarely took a day off. We were up early tending to the needs of the guests and didn't go to bed until the last guest left the lodge. The guests expected our full attention and we provided it. After one particularly busy week, we decided to take the night off. We were scheduled to pick guests up at the airport in Billings, Montana on Sunday. Saturday morning as the last guests departed the Ranch, we gathered a few things and headed off the mountain. We decided to make reservations in Red Lodge, Montana. We drove to Red Lodge via the Chief Joseph Scenic Byway and the Beartooth Highway which took us through the Shoshone National Forest across the Absaroka Mountains. It was a beautiful day with bright blue skies and the mountain air was fresh and crisp as we drove the Beartooth Pass with an elevation of 10,947 feet.

Red Lodge is a small scenic western town only 2.6 square miles in size and a population of 2,114 inhabitants. Bill and I were looking forward to a quiet, peaceful day in Red Lodge. As we drove off the mountain and drove into Red Lodge, there was a large banner hanging overhead across the street. The banner read, *Welcome to the Iron Horse Rodeo.* Much to our dismay, we had chosen a weekend when Red Lodge was hosting a bike rally. There were ten thousand Harleys in town for the weekend. Everywhere we looked, there were motorcycles. Bill and I looked at each other in disbelief! So much for our quiet get-away!

The bed and breakfast where we made our reservation is located a few streets away from the downtown where most of the festivities were taking place. As we walked to the downtown restaurant for an early dinner, I said to Bill, "The first t-shirt that comes off and we're out of here!" Much to our pleasure dinner was enjoyable and the bikers that we met were commonplace people who were respectful, fun loving people just out for a good time. After dinner we spent the evening on the front porch of the bed and breakfast enjoying a quiet evening in this quaint little town.

Cody, Wyoming, was one of Bill and I's favorite places to visit. During the summer season we brought our guests to Cody every Thursday afternoon for shopping and attended the Cody Nite Rodeo with the guests in the evening. Many times between seasons and whenever possible during the season we visited Cody and on occasion stayed at the historic Irma Hotel. The Irma Hotel, named after his daughter, was built by Buffalo Bill Cody in 1902. The famous cherry bar given as a gift to Buffalo Bill Cody by Queen Victoria is a focal point of the dining room located in the Irma Hotel.

Over time, we became friends with many of the business owners in Cody and enjoyed stopping to talk with them during our visits. The business owners relied on the tourist industry for their business and appreciated the guests that our ranch, along with the many other guest ranches in the area, brought to Cody.

Living in the Big Horn Mountains provided many unique experiences. Along with the everyday appearance of moose, the evening stars remain one of my greatest pleasures. The appearance of the stars in the evening was an incredible image. Due to the high elevation, clean air, and little light pollution, the stars were visible in the millions and appeared as large as street lights in many instances. I remember standing with guests for what seemed like hours after our Friday evening campfire soaking in the remarkable night sky covered in millions of sparkling stars. And, on occasion we were entertained by the Northern Lights which danced across the Wyoming skies. I remember being awakened during the night by Kayleen, one of our first wranglers, to experience the Northern Lights for the first time.

The climate on the mountain provided a few learning experiences. Our first summer at the Ranch, I prepared a flower garden at the entrance to the lodge and attempted to grow flowers from seeds. Due to the cooler and shorter growing season, my flowers only grew to about two inches tall. I learned that pansies are very hardy and about the only flowers that would stay alive on the mountain, other than the wildflowers. And, the pumpkins I used to decorate with in September froze solid after a few days.

Altitude sickness was one of the learning experiences that we dealt with often. The Ranch sat at 8,300 feet and we often rode horses at elevations of 9,300 feet. Altitude sickness most often occurs at elevations above 8,000 feet. Feelings of fatigue, dizziness, headaches, feeling jittery, and nausea generally are signs of altitude sickness. At the high altitudes, there is less oxygen in the air which also contributes to dehydration. We found that guests that drank lots of coffee generally were the ones that most often suffered from altitude sickness. We encouraged our guests to drink plenty of water during their visit which helped alleviate altitude sickness.

Due to the dry climate in the West, wildfires were ever present during the summer months. Even though there were several wildfires in the Big Horns during our ownership of the Ranch, thankfully, they were far enough away that we were not severely threatened by them. Although in 2001, Montana had severe wildfires and the smoke from those fires hung in the Big Horns. The smoke would be thick enough to block our view of the mountains in front of the Ranch. And you could actually taste the smoke as you walked out of the lodge, especially in the morning. Although the threat of wildfires was worrisome, the effect from the smoke provided some exquisite sunsets.

The drive up the mountain from either side was picturesque and lush during the summer months as a result of the winter snowfall. From the west, you drove up Shell Canyon. Granite rock formations were plentiful and full of color. The road wound thru the canyon which followed the path formed by Shell Creek. In the fall, groves of brilliant golden Aspen trees were sprinkled throughout the acres of green pines. Also in the fall, the road was often lined with cattle following one another in single formation for miles down the mountain as the cowboys drove them off the mountain. I always loved watching the cattle as they sauntered down the road through Shell Canyon. For me, it was part of the experience of living in the West. I think that is why I was so bewildered at hearing comments from a tourist one day upon stopping at Shell Falls. She was complaining to the forest ranger about the cows on the road and how they impeded the traffic flow and how bad they smelled. My feelings of dismay subsided and changed to pity as I learned she called Manhattan home.

Another experience that was new to us was buying weed-free hay for the horses. In an attempt to keep noxious weeds from being introduced up on the mountain, the forest service had a long standing regulation that weed-free hay was the only hay that was permitted on the mountain. Ranchers off the mountain would have their hay inspected and if permitted could sell the hay as "weed-free." They had to bale the hay using a multicolored baling twine which designated it as weed-free. After checking with the county extension agent, Shane and I drove down to Shell to attempt to find weed-free hay to buy for our horses. Loren Good was on the list and after locating his ranch in Shell, we followed instructions from his wife Margie where we could find him. Loren confirmed that he had weed-free hay and agreed to sell us a truck load full. He also offered to deliver a hay wagon full of hay to the Ranch the next week. Meeting Loren and Margie was one of the joys of living near Shell. Loren and Margie had grown up and raised their own family in the area and are some of the nicest people that a person could ever meet. Loren continued to sell us hay until several years later when he stopped making hay and then he offered the use of his wagon to pick up hay whenever the need arose.

Margie attended the small church in Shell and invited Bill and I to attend with her. Although we regularly attended church in Ohio, it was difficult for us to get away during our three guest seasons to attend church in Wyoming. Between seasons we started attending the small non-denominational church located in Shell. The church was a quaint little building with a sanctuary that was about the size of the great room in our lodge. The minister was a circuit minister who traveled from one church to another on Sunday morning giving the sermon. Often when Bill and I attended the church, we increased the size of the congregation by twenty percent. Nevertheless, we enjoyed attending church in Shell whenever possible.

Healthcare in the area was provided by the clinic that was located in Basin, just outside Greybull. Fortunately, we only visited the clinic on rare occasions with the occurrence of a cold or flu. The clinic was small and refreshing due to the fact that you seldom waited to be seen. Instead of a doctor, you were diagnosed and treated by a nurse practitioner.

Late one afternoon, shortly before dinner, I was taking a shower and was interrupted by a frantic knock on the door. Soaking wet, I answered the nervous calls to come quickly, Bill had been injured. I quickly dried off and dressed. Billy and Bill had been splitting wood behind the lodge. As Bill stood waiting his turn to use the axe, Billy swung the axe toward the next waiting block of wood. Suddenly, the axe head came loose from the handle and whirled off in the air landing in the side of Bill's boot. Fortunately, Bill was wearing his heavy leather boots, but the sharp axe head sliced through the leather and cut into Bill's foot. Blood spurted from his foot as Bill gently removed his boot. The wranglers had all acted quickly gathering towels to wrap Bill's bleeding foot and preparing the Suburban for our ride down the mountain to the clinic. One of the wranglers had even called the clinic to make them aware of our impending arrival and circumstance.

The drive to Basin is usually a good hour drive. That day, I made the drive in thirty minutes as Bill propped his foot up on the dash of the Suburban to help control the bleeding. I figured if I was stopped by the Sheriff, he would see the need to hurry and would probably escort me to the clinic. As we arrived at the clinic and entered the doors, the awaiting nurse escorted us through the clinic as she flipped on the lights. Even in the afternoon, in this small town the clinic was seldom busy. The nurse practitioner quickly placed fourteen stitches in Bill's foot explaining that he was rather lucky at the thickness of the leather in his boot and the near miss of cutting an adjacent tendon.

The months of April, November, and early December were our downtime at the Ranch. The weather in April, although still snowing, didn't provide enough snow to continue snowmobiling; and our usual snowmobilers were ready to put their snowmobiles away and begin thinking about spring weather and other outdoor sports. Following hunting season for elk in early November up until late December, the mountain was quiet. Bill and I took advantage of these times of the year to travel back to Ohio to visit our kids and other family. Traveling back to Ohio during these months sometimes provided some extreme traveling conditions brought on by the weather.

On one such trip, Bill was transporting five colts and one of our ranch horses back to our son Brandon, who lived in Virginia. We planned to leave early in the morning and awoke to seventeen inches of fresh snow on the mountain. The weather report predicted a snow storm on the northern route through South Dakota, so Bill decided to take the Southern route across Wyoming and Nebraska. Our trip started with picking up the colts at our property located in Shell. After loading the colts, we proceeded south through the Wind River Canyon. The snow continued falling throughout the day, and although we experienced few problems, travel was slow, and we were only able to drive to Nebraska before stopping for the night.

The second day of the trip, the weather conditions worsened as we drove through an ice storm. Numerous cars and trucks had driven off the road and were stuck along the way as we proceeded through Nebraska. The driving was slow and intense, and on a few occasions cars would pass us and then slide off the road as they attempted to pull back over in front of us. It was a long day and we were still in Nebraska when we decided to stop for the night. Bill had to chip ice off the hay, which was strapped to the outside of the horse trailer, in order to feed the horses.

The third day we continued through heavy snow but had made the decision to drive through to Bill's brother's house in Ohio before stopping for the night. Bill had called Randy and asked him to find some hay as the delay in travel caused us to run short on hay for the horses.

On the fourth day we left Ohio and headed to Virginia. The weather had improved and we were planning for an easy day of driving. About an hour and a half from our destination, a tire on the horse trailer blew and as we pulled over to work on the tire, it started pouring down rain. Changing a tire on a horse trailer carrying six horses in pouring rain proved to be a challenging experience. Once the tire was changed, we continued on our way only to encounter another flat tire a few miles down the highway. Eventually and to our delight, we arrived at our destination shortly before dark. Those six horses were equally happy when we unloaded them from the trailer.

Sharing the Ranch with our family was another of our greatest pleasures. Many family members helped out during the renovation of the cabins and the painting of the lodge and cabins. Bill's mom and dad not only helped during the renovation stage, but also came almost every year for a week or so to visit. My mom visited the Ranch the first summer season. As we were driving up the mountain, I pointed to the high mountain meadow to show her about where the Ranch sat. She thought I was teasing but soon found out that I was not. Mom was not fond of the ride up the mountain roads to the Ranch, but once at the Ranch enjoyed the quiet peaceful nature.

My sister, Marlene, and her husband, Jim, were regulars during the summer. I enjoyed Marlene's visits not only for the help in the kitchen, but especially for the company and conversation during the busy days. Marlene was not able to trail ride, but Bill ponied her around the pasture. Jim, on the other hand, thoroughly enjoyed riding the horses along with the guests and wranglers. Jim is tall and teased that he cleared all the spider webs along the trails for the other guests.

Marlene was visiting the Ranch the year that my brother, Tim, passed away. Tim was just a year older than I and lost his battle with cancer the day before my birthday. I had spent time with Tim during our visits to Ohio and was saddened by his death. The decision not to go back to Ohio for my brother's funeral made it even harder to deal with the loss I felt. Having my sister there at the Ranch during this time meant everything to me. While Bill took me on a long horseback ride that day to help me have some alone time to grieve my brother's passing, Marlene stayed behind and arranged for a granite boulder to be moved from behind the cabins to my flower garden as a tribute to Tim. She and I laid flowers at the base of the boulder as a memorial of his life and the love we felt for him.

Bill's brother, Randy, and his wife, Patty, also visited often. One of Bill's favorite stories to tell was of taking Patty across the ridge above the Ranch on horseback. Knowing that Patty was fearful of heights, Bill started preparing her ahead of time that once they came to a certain point that she would want to stay close behind his horse and keep her eyes on him. As the trail opened with the vast view of Shell Canyon that lay below it, Bill could hear Patty's nervous gasps and occasional sniffles. She adhered to Bill's advice following him across the ridge and safely into the forest that lay in front of them.

Bill's cousin Michelle and Sean came to visit in late August, early September. It was nice to spend some quality time with Michelle and Sean and get to know them on a more personal level. Michelle stayed for three weeks and helped out around the Ranch with cabin cleaning and in the kitchen, when needed.

Several nieces and nephews were among those that visited and we always enjoyed showing them around the Ranch and sharing the ranch activities with them.

I have never been a great lover of indoor cats, but let me put it this way; I like cats more than I like mice. The remote location of the Ranch seemed to necessitate the need for an indoor cat. Missy and I loaded a large box in the back of the Suburban and headed off the mountain to a farm where we often picked up hay. The owner of the farm had told me to stop by anytime and pick up a few kittens as he had an abundance of kittens to choose from. I had been to this farm many times, but Missy was amazed and amused as we drove up to the house to see cats and kittens coming from everywhere. There must have been fifty of them peering from under the porch, peeking from out buildings and running around the yard. All of these cats were kept outdoors and the majority of them were not domesticated.

Carson greeted us from the porch and offered to catch a few of the kittens for us. We attempted to choose a few for him to catch, but finally settled on *whatever* he could catch. Those kittens were quick! They were also mean as they scratched and hissed whenever he came close. It was a good thing that we brought a deep box with a lid because those kittens were out of the box in an instant before we could even get the lid closed, hissing and scratching the entire time. After about forty-five minutes, Carson was able to catch two kittens and secure them in the box for the ride home. Missy and I were a little nervous at the thought of those mean little critters escaping inside the Suburban during the ride home and took Carson up on his offer to tape the lid closed for us.

Back at the Ranch, Missy and I carefully carried the box into the lodge and attempted to put some food and water in the box with the kittens. Within a short time those kittens escaped the box and were running loose around the kitchen. What took place next is both embarrassing and comical. These two kittens which were only weeks old and slightly larger than a slice of bread had Missy and I trapped on the top of the kitchen table like two scaredy-cats. Each time we attempted to retrieve them or move them with the broom they hissed and clawed like savage beasts. Here I am, a strong woman who had prided herself on surviving several years of living on a mountain in a remote area of Wyoming and I was afraid of two kittens. Missy and I could see the humor in the situation, but also remained on the table until Bill got back from a trail ride and put the kittens outside.

Over the next few weeks Missy and I both attempted to befriend the kittens and were slowly able to gain their trust and calm their savage ways. One of the kittens was grey and white and the other was yellow and white striped. We named the grey kitten Mallow Cat and the yellow one KitKat. The kittens were adjusting to life on the Ranch and Cali and Lucy were getting accustomed to them. The dogs were no match for these two feisty kittens who could fend for themselves and gave both dogs a few scratches on the nose in the process.

Unfortunately, the grey kitten went missing and KitKat was moved to the inside of the lodge. She grew accustomed to living indoors although she could go outdoors during the day and went about the business of catching mice. She was very proud of her skills and, much to my dismay, was excited to bring her catch to me for praise.

KitKat was fun to watch as she playfully entertained herself in the lodge by darting up the log stair rails and running across the high log beams that extended through the top of the great room. She was quiet and unobtrusive and a fun addition to the Ranch pets.

With all the wonderful experiences while living on the mountain at the Ranch, it is difficult to think about the more unpleasant aspects. Bill and I lived in the lodge. Our only private space was our bedroom which was above the kitchen. We even shared the bathroom which was on the main floor of the lodge, behind the kitchen. During the guest season, it was difficult and sometimes impossible to have any alone time. Oftentimes on Tuesday evening during line dancing night (an activity put on by the staff), Bill and I would take a walk just to have a few minutes to discuss ideas or talk over issues that had arisen, or just to spend some time together. We had on occasion resorted to jumping in the Suburban and driving up the road to discuss more heated topics. With the closeness of the staff and the inability to have separate quarters away from the lodge, this became a real issue.

The other more heart wrenching issue of operating a guest ranch is the ever present risk of a guest being hurt. Although we had a few occurrences of guests coming off their horses, there were a few guests who suffered broken ribs. Although painful, the guests were able to quickly recover from these issues. On one occasion, however, a horse flipped over, landing on its young rider which resulted in the necessity of the young person being flown to a nearby hospital for treatment. Although this young person spent most of the week in the hospital she fully recovered. Regardless, Bill and I felt horrible. We would have felt badly regardless of whom it was, but this young person and her family are dear friends. Bill and I both took the safety of our guests very seriously but also took full responsibility whenever anything of this nature happened.

The Final Chapter

The decision to sell the Ranch did not come easily. Bill and I talked about the pros and cons of selling the Ranch for months before settling on the final decision. Bill and I both loved the Ranch but honestly the loneliness of living on the Ranch, especially during the long winter months, and the constant longing to be closer to my family made my decision easier. For Bill the decision was much harder. Those close to Bill could understand his reluctance, as he was living his dream.

The final decision was made easier for us by the birth of our granddaughter. Emma was born in December of 2002. Missy and Emma were able to spend some time with us during her first year, but once they were back in Ohio, Bill and I both missed seeing her on a regular basis. It was heartbreaking for me when we went home to Ohio to visit and Emma hardly remembered who we were. And, Brandon and Jess were now making plans to start their family.

Shane was usually able to visit us at the Ranch for at least a week with his friends, but a week with my son just wasn't enough. And, as Missy and Brandon became busier with their own families, it became increasingly more difficult for them to visit us at all. Also, as our parents aged, we really needed to be closer to them to help out when needed.

In addition to family concerns, the economy was just starting to take a sharp decline. Gas prices were climbing and although our business continued to thrive, the guest ranch industry and the tourism business as a whole was beginning to feel the pinch.

Once the final decision was made, we contacted both Tom Sharpe, our realtor and friend in Colorado, and Bob Bole, our local realtor and friend in Wyoming, and the process of listing and showing the Ranch began.

Bill and I continued on with business as usual. We understood that this process would take some time and were comfortable throughout the process, determined to enjoy our remaining days of owning and living at the Ranch. Our core staff had worked for us previous years and we talked with them as soon as the decision was made to sell the Ranch. They, of course, were sad at the thought of us selling the Ranch but were extremely understanding about our reasons for wanting to move back to Ohio.

Bill and I talked at length about our employment plans once we returned to Ohio. My experience was in the legal field and I was anxious to return to a career in that area. It's funny, when we were planning to purchase the Ranch the idea of wearing jeans to work every day was very appealing to me. Now, I was looking forward to wearing business attire once again. And, the thought of losing the responsibility of feeding upwards of twenty-five people each and every meal was looking even more appealing.

Bill desired to remain in the entertainment business and began researching the idea of starting a business owning an entertainment venue, specializing in horse related, western events. He and our wrangler, Billy, talked at length about the possibilities available to this type of venue. Bill continued to make necessary contacts in the business and looked at possible locations for the venue during our visits to Ohio.

Several serious buyers visited the Ranch over the next year and a few proposals were submitted. One offer was withdrawn after learning firsthand the difficulty working with the Forest Service. But by fall of 2004, we thought we had a concrete offer. And, although we still had not closed on the offer to purchase, we made the decision to move our personal belongs and furniture back to Ohio in late October. We knew if we didn't move our things before the deep snow fell, we would have to wait until early summer before we could drive back into the Ranch.

Boxing up our belongings and going through the items at the Ranch was difficult. So many memories were created and those items were reminders of those wonderful memories. Once again, although we were excited about our future plans, we were leaving behind a place and time that we had grown to love.

Josh, a friend from Shell, and my brother, Rusty, came out to help us move our belongings. Over a few days Bill, Rusty, and Josh loaded a moving truck with our belongings as I cleaned the lodge behind them. After the last box was loaded, Bill and Rusty loaded the horses into our horse trailer and Rusty's horse trailer for the trip back to Ohio.

As was normal for this time of year, it had snowed several inches the night before we were to leave. Josh had to park his car halfway down the road leading up to the Ranch due to the snowfall. Bill decided that I would drive the moving truck and he would drive our Suburban pulling the horse trailer. I had never driven a moving truck before and I was a little nervous, but I didn't really have a choice, so I climbed into the moving truck and, along with Josh, headed down the road. It had started snowing again and a few inches of new snow added to the snowfall from the previous night.

I drove slow as I headed down the steep, narrow mountain road and tried to appear confident in front of Josh, but was feeling increasingly nervous as we drew closer to Josh's car parked alongside the road. I noticed that the moving truck felt top heavy and with the added slickness of the new snow, didn't really want to stop when I applied pressure to the brakes. Now, as we were within a few yards of Josh's car and the truck was sliding as I tried to stop, I couldn't hide my nervousness and the look on Josh's face revealed that he was thinking the same thing I was thinking, *I'm going to hit Josh's car.* Within a few inches of Josh's car, the tires finally hit a clear place in the gravel road and the tires took hold stopping just in time. With a look of bewilderment in his eyes, Josh looked over at me and asked, "Are you going to be all right driving this truck down the mountain?" Although not sure of my answer I said, "I'll be fine!"

The drive down the mountain from the Ranch to Sheridan was slippery with the new snow. After stopping in Sheridan for dinner, we made the decision to stay the night in Sheridan and start out again in the morning.

Bill and I had made this drive from the Ranch to Ohio for over eight years now and usually it took two long days. Even with the added effort of pulling a horse trailer, we were planning on two and a half days at the most to complete the trip. We didn't even imagine the trials that lay ahead of us.

Bill led the caravan, driving the Suburban pulling the horse trailer. I followed along with the moving truck and Rusty brought up the rear in his truck pulling his horse trailer. Bill had five horses in the stock trailer (Baldy, Duke, Ranger, Oak, and Lacey), and Rusty had Sadie and the colt in his horse trailer. Kit Kat was in her carrier in the front seat of my truck and Lucy and Cali were riding with Bill. We had discussed that if a problem arose or we needed to exit for any reason, the person would flash their lights and Bill would know to pull over. We all had cell phones, but the reception in this part of the country was spotty and wasn't always reliable.

Driving through the flat, wide open spaces of Wyoming posed few problems. As we drove through South Dakota, suddenly I saw something fly off of our horse trailer and smoke began billowing from the tire. As directed, I started flashing my lights and honking my horn for Bill to pull over. Bill didn't react and finally I decided to pass Bill and flag him to pull over. Upon inspection, Bill and Rusty discovered that the leaf spring had snapped on the horse trailer causing the bed of the trailer to drop onto the axle which made the wheel rub on the fender. Bill and Rusty worked to jack up the trailer with the scissor jack until it suddenly broke under the pressure causing a bolt to fly out of the jack, just missing the guys. Using a hydraulic jack this time they once again jacked up the bed of the trailer and propped it in place with a 4 x 4 piece of wood. Limping slowly down the road, we were able to drive to Wall Drug and quickly located a welder. After unloading the five horses, the welder began the process of welding the leaf spring back in place. This process took most of the afternoon and after loading and reshuffling the horses, we drove to Chamberlain, South Dakota, along the Missouri River where we spent the night.

Day three of our trip started out fine, but mid-morning Bill started having trouble with the Suburban. He pulled over a couple of times as the electrical system intermittently stopped functioning causing the lights, blinkers, and radio to stop working. Shortly after pulling off the expressway in Sioux City, South Dakota, we located a mechanic. After unloading the horses again, the mechanic began the work of replacing the alternator. After lunch, the mechanic came to Bill to explain that although he had replaced the alternator, he busted a hose in the process and would need to replace it.

By the time we left Sioux City, it was getting late and it had started to rain. Bill again had to pull over as the windshield wipers on the Suburban were not working. We slowly made our way to Des Moines, Iowa, where we spent the night.

The next day it wasn't raining and we were able to drive, without complications to Indianapolis before stopping for the night. The following morning as we prepared to leave the motel, Bill pulled the Suburban with the horse trailer forward in the parking lot and jumped out of the truck motioning me toward the entrance. As I sat in the moving truck and watched him motioning to me, I noticed that the Suburban and horse trailer were slowly drifting backwards. In his haste to direct me, he had neglected to put the Suburban in gear. As the Suburban and horse trailer continued to drift backwards, I began to yell and flail my arms to draw his attention to what was happening behind him. Rusty was doing the same from inside his truck which was parked next to me. Completely unaware of what was happening behind him; his face displayed a puzzled look to the antics displayed by both Rusty and me as he could not hear what we were yelling. Finally and just in the nick of time, he turned around to realize the truck was no longer behind him. He dashed for the Suburban and jumped inside, stopping the truck just before it hit the opened car door directly in its path. The man standing between the opened car door and his car was frozen in fear as his wide eyes witnessed the impending danger.

We finally arrived in Ohio on day five of our trip. Bill and Rusty took the horses to Rusty's farm in Norwich and I drove the moving truck to Gahanna where we had leased a house. Missy had located a house for us to lease in Gahanna for the interim period while we sold the Ranch and decided where we wanted to purchase property.

I had already started applying for jobs and even did a telephone interview with the Ohio Secretary of State's Office during a lunch stop on our trip back from

Wyoming. Although, in the end, I did not get the job, I did get a second in-person interview for the position. With the help of a temporary employment agency, I worked temporary jobs until I was able to get a permanent, full time job at the corporate office of State Farm Insurance.

Bill remained in Ohio until mid-December and then headed back to the Ranch. The previous purchase offer fell through and Bill remained at the Ranch during snowmobile season. I still helped Bill with reservations from Ohio via the computer, but worried about Bill at the Ranch, sometimes alone, during the winter months. Another offer to purchase quickly came along, however, and Bill worked with the interested party throughout the winter months. Shortly after closing on the purchase offer in the spring, Bill returned to Ohio. Part of the agreement to purchase included Bill coming back to the Ranch in June to help acclimate the new owners to the area and familiarize them with the Ranch.

Bill and Billy, one of our previous wranglers, traveled to the Ranch and assisted the new owners in purchasing some equipment, making some repairs and familiarizing them with the trails and the area around the Ranch.

As Bill and Billy were taking Andre on a trail ride to show him the lunch ride, a storm appeared to be brewing off in the distance. Andre had to stop several times to adjust his saddle, delaying their advance along the trail. The leased horses had just been delivered the previous day and all three of the guys were riding horses with which they were not familiar. After stopping again to talk to a wrangler from another guest ranch, suddenly the weather took a considerable turn for the worst and it started hailing, the sky had turned pitch black, and the wind was whipping. Not knowing how these particular horses would deal with the elements, Bill motioned that they would make a run back toward the Ranch. As they started galloping down the trail, the wind sounded like a train coming through the trees and the trees cracked as they started falling around them. One tree after another snapped off falling in their path and as they made their way up the trail toward the Ranch. As they neared the clearing in the trees a huge pine tree had been uprooted and lay sideways, with the roots sticking twelve feet out of the ground.

Soaking wet, but safely back at the Ranch, Bill and Billy told Andre that after they tended to the horses and cleaned up they would drive down to Dirty Annie's for dinner. As they walked into Dirty Annie's, Jim, the owner, commented, "Did you guys see the tornado that took place on the mountain?"

The next morning as they were riding the breakfast ride with Andre, Bill and Billy came upon an area just above the pasture where the grove of trees had all been blown down. Hundreds of trees looked like pick-up sticks as they lay on the ground. As they continued their ride up the dirt road and toward Eagles Nest, another grove of trees was blown down the opposite direction. The tornado had evidently spiraled and blown the trees down in its path.

Bill returned to Ohio and although the venture to open an entertainment center in Ohio didn't work out, he eventually went to work for an accounting firm in

Worthington, Ohio, where he is now a partner. He
began riding his horse as a civil war re-enactor with the
6th Ohio Calvary. This helped fulfill his desire to ride
horses and his love of history.

After a year and a half at State Farm Insurance, I
returned to my career as a legal assistant with The
Department of Justice in the Office of the US Trustee
in downtown Columbus, Ohio.

Over the years since we returned to Ohio, we have
told and retold stories of our experiences while owning
and living at Ranger Creek Guest Ranch. Our journey
to the Ranch began with our son's battle with cancer.
Because of Brandon's battle with cancer, Bill and I were
able to let go of our control over our lives and take a leap
of faith in pursuing the dream of owning the Ranch.
Our priorities changed and we were able to see beyond
our comfort zone. Purchasing and living at the Ranch,
in a remote location, on a mountain in Wyoming, was
far beyond our comfort zone. Snowmobiling into the
Ranch in the wintertime and sharing the Ranch with
wildlife such as moose, bear, and mountain lion was
abnormal to our usual way of life. We learned to rely on
God and each other and we learned that we were able
to deal with forces of nature that were far beyond what
were normal and natural to us in Ohio.

The peaceful nature of the Ranch helped us to
heal from the struggles that led to this place. The
quietness of the mountain, the exquisite brilliance of
the night sky, and the miles of breathtaking purple
wildflowers helped us remember the tender goodness
of a loving God. The sheer pleasure of living among the

wildlife and the respect that we felt for these animals reminded us on a daily basis how thankful we were for having been permitted this experience.

Our lives were forever changed by the experience of meeting and sharing the Ranch with the children who attended the Ranch Rodeo. These children who have suffered through treatment for many different illnesses possess courage beyond their young years. They were a joy to meet and a reminder of how fragile life is. If for no other reason than the opportunity to bring a little joy into their world, our journey was worth the price.

Bill and I both still feel privileged to have known and shared our lives with the staff that worked for us at the Ranch. These young men and women gave so much of themselves and we are so very thankful to have known them.

As we share pictures of the Ranch with others in Ohio, sometimes I wonder, do they think it's not so great? But when I look at the pictures I see more than a picture. I see the memories of the staff, the guests, the horses, and all the fun times that we shared during those precious years of owning the Ranch. Bill and I feel honored to have been given the unique privilege of living on and owning the Ranch.

My continual prayer is that Ranger Creek Guest Ranch, with its unique character and peaceful nature, will continue to touch the lives of those who are blessed to walk on its hallowed ground for years to come. I truly hope that I will be able to return to Ranger Creek Guest Ranch some day with my grandchildren and share some of these special memories with them.

Until that day, God bless you and God bless a pretty day and a safe day on the mountain. Amen.

Bill and I

Brandon, Missy, and Shane

Ranch Recipes

Recipes were given to me by staff members, guests, and family. Listed below are just a few of the Ranch favorites:

Chicken Divan

2 10 oz. pkg. frozen broccoli (cooked)
1 t. lemon juice
2 c. cubed cooked chicken breast
2 oz. shredded cheddar cheese
3/4 c. mayo
1 c. soft bread crumbs
1 can cream of chicken
1 T. melted butter

Arrange cooked and drained broccoli in the bottom of a greased 9 x 12 casserole dish. Layer cubed chicken on top. Combine soup, mayo, and lemon juice. Spread over chicken and sprinkle with cheese. Place bread crumbs on top and sprinkle with butter. Bake at 350 degrees for 35 minutes or until bread crumbs are slightly browned.

Since Wild Bill doesn't like many vegetables, I would make two dishes of Chicken Divan and substitute the layer of broccoli with a layer of cooked white rice.

Sopapilla

Filling Mix: Prepare First
1 1/2 lbs. ground beef
1 pkg. taco seasoning mix
1 large onion – chopped (optional)

Cook and drain; return to pan and add 1 package taco seasoning mix and 1/2 cup of water. Cook 15 minutes. Let the mixture cool while preparing dough.

Dough Mix:
1 pkg. yeast   3 T. vegetable oil
1 1/2 c. warm water   4 c. flour
2 T. sugar   2 eggs
1 1/2 t. salt

Will also need: shredded cheddar & mozzarella cheese
   Mix together yeast and water. Add sugar, salt, eggs, oil, and flour one at a time. Pinch dough into balls. Roll dough balls into circles on floured surface. Fill with cooled hamburger mixture. Add shredded cheddar and mozzarella cheese. Fold one edge of circle over mixture and pinch the edges to seal in the mixture. Be sure there are no openings or holes. Deep fry in hot oil, turning once, until golden brown. Drain on paper towels and keep warm in oven.
   Serve with shredded lettuce, diced tomatoes, shredded cheese, sour cream, and salsa.

Bacon, Eggs, & Cheese Casserole

Serves 8

1/2 lb. bacon	6 eggs
6 slices white bread	2 c. milk
1/2 lb. processed cheese	1/2 t. salt
1/4 t. dry mustard	

Cut bacon in small pieces and fry until crisp. Cut bread slices in cubes and place in greased 9 x 13 casserole dish. Cube or shred cheese and layer on top of bread. Mix eggs, milk, salt, and dry mustard. Pour over bread and cheese. Sprinkle bacon pieces on top. Cover and refrigerate overnight. Bake covered at 350 degrees for 50-60 minutes or until puffed up and slightly browned. Serve immediately.

May substitute ground sausage or ham for bacon.

Best Dinner Rolls

Makes 2 dozen

1 pkg. yeast	1/3 c. margarine
1/2 c. warm water	1/3 c. sugar
1 t. sugar	Dash of salt
1 t. baking powder	2 beaten eggs
1 c. milk	4 1/2 c. flour

Dissolve yeast in warm water. Add sugar and baking powder. Let sit 20 minutes. Scald milk and add margarine, sugar, and salt. Cool and then add eggs. Add to yeast mixture. Mix in flour. Cover and refrigerate overnight. Roll out 2 hours before serving and shape either as butter horns or pinwheels in well-greased muffin tins. Let rise until double. Bake at 400 degrees for 10-15 minutes. Brush with melted butter.

Strawberry Lettuce Salad

Serves 8 – 10
Dressing:
1/3 c. Red Wine Vinegar
1 t. salt
1/2 c. sugar
1 t. dried mustard
1/4 c. oil
1 1/2 T. poppy seeds

Combine the above ingredients, shaking well before adding to salad.

1 head Romaine lettuce
1 pint strawberries*
1 bag spinach
1/2 c. toasted pecans or chopped walnuts

Prepare lettuce and top with strawberries and toasted pecans. Top with dressing and serve.

*Even though this is called a Strawberry salad, I rarely added the strawberries. It was one of my personal favorites as well as the staff and the guests.

Wild Bill's Raisin Sauce

1/4 c. sugar
1 T. cornstarch
1 c. water
2 c. raisins

Combine sugar and cornstarch in saucepan. Stir in 1 cup water and raisins. Cook over medium heat until thick and bubbly. Let cool. Serve over ham or as a side.

Poppy Seed Biscuit Ring

(Second most requested recipe)
1/3 c. butter (melted)
1 t. dried minced onion
1 t. poppy seeds
1/2 t. dried minced garlic
2 tubes (12 oz. each) refrigerated buttermilk biscuits

In a bowl, combine melted butter, onion, poppy seeds and garlic. Separate each tube of biscuits and dip in butter mixture. Stand on end in a lightly greased 10 inch fluted tube pan.

Bake at 400 degrees for 14-16 minutes or until golden brown. Immediately invert onto a serving plate. Serve warm.

Another variation of this recipe is to dip the biscuits in butter, then cinnamon and sugar and bake as directed above.

Wild Bill's Banana Dessert

2 pkgs. Graham crackers
1 stick butter
4 bananas
2 (3 oz.) pkgs. Vanilla pudding
1/2 c. milk
1 quart vanilla ice cream
1 small container cool whip

Crush graham crackers, add melted butter. Press in 9 x 13 pan. Reserve a few crumbs for top of dessert.

Slice bananas over crust. Mix pudding with milk until set, add ice cream, and cool whip. Pour over bananas. Sprinkle with remaining crumbs. Refrigerate until ready to serve – about one hour.

Apple Dump Cake

(Most requested recipe)
2 cans apple* pie filling
1 stick butter
1 box yellow cake mix

Spread pie filling on the bottom of a 9 x 13 pan. Spread the entire box of dry cake mix over the top. Slice the stick of butter and lay on top of the cake mix. Bake at 350 degrees for 20 minutes until the top is lightly browned.

Serve warm with ice cream.

*Cherry, peach, and rhubarb pie filling is also very good

Chocolate Chip Marsh Mellow Bars

(Third most requested recipe)
1 c. shortening
1 t. salt
3/4 c. brown sugar
1 t. baking soda
3/4 c. white sugar
1 c. chopped nuts (optional)
2 eggs
3/4 c. chocolate chips
1 t. vanilla
2 c. miniature marsh mellows
2 1/4 c. flour

Combine shortening and sugars, beat until creamy. Beat eggs and vanilla; gradually add flour, salt, and baking soda. Stir in nuts, chocolate chips, and marsh mellows. Spread in 9 x 11 greased pan. Bake at 375 degrees for 20 minutes until the top is lightly browned. Let set a few minutes before cutting.

Articles Published About Ranger Creek Guest Ranch

"Comisfords Purchase Ranger Creek Guest Ranch." *The Sheridan Press,* November 20, 1999.

Jim Morris. "Numbers Man in the Saddle." *The Dayton Daily News,* April 4, 1999.

Cassie Holderham. "Saddling Up, Heading West." *The Advocate,* sec. 3A, April 10, 1999.

Wyeth Friday. "Ohio Family Reopens Ranch." *The Sheridan Press,* pg. 7, August 29, 1999.

Larque Richter. "Cancer Retreat Offers Relief." *The Sheridan Press,* pg. 1, September 14, 1999.

Larque Richter. "Retreat Gives Girl Chance to be a Kid." *The Sheridan Press,* pg. 2, September 15, 1999.

"Privileged to be Part of Rodeo." *The Sheridan Press,* September 15, 1999.

Jade Smith. "Welcome Bill, Sue, Brandon Comisford." *Greybull Standard,* September 16, 1999.

Marilyn Good. "Ohio 'City Slickers' take to ranchin' life." *Greybull Standard,* September 23, 1999.

Marlboro Reisen. (2000). Amerika.

Peter Fox. "Big Air in the Big Horns." *Powder Magazine*, pg. 28, February, 2001.

"Bill Comisford '76." *Ohio State Alumni Magazine*, pg. 38, March 2000.

Larque Richter. "Respite Rodeo Draws 12 Youth and Families." *The Sheridan Press*, pg. 1, June 28, 2000.

Larque Richter. "Mountain Retreat Gives Youth Battling Terminal Illnesses a Reason to Smile." *The Sheridan County Roundup*, pg.3, July 5, 2000.

Lisa Reuter. "Life's Long View." *The Columbus Dispatch*, sec. F, July 9, 2000.

"Buckeye Dudes." *Ohio State Alumni Magazine*, November 2000.

Lauren Bernstein. "Great Family-Reunion Getaways." *Parents Magazine*, Travel News pg. 211, July 2000.

Gene Kilgore. *Ranch Vacations*, California: Avalon Travel, 2001

Markus Wolf. "A Horse and a Sky- That's all Tanja Heck Needs to be Happy." *Maxi Magazine*, pg. 102-106, December 2001.

Argus Reisen. (2001). *Ranch and Adventure Holidays.*

Jade Smith. "Ranch Hosts Fifth Annual Make-A-Smile Rodeo." *Greybull Standard*, June 26, 2003.

Sally Ann Shurmur. "Ranger Creek Guest Ranch Makes Wishes Come True." *Star Tribune Casper Inside*, sec. C, July 18, 2003.

CPSIA information can be obtained at www.ICGtesting.com
Printed in the USA
LVOW04s2039010914

401885LV00032B/1331/P